This book is dedicated to Leo and Anne Panas, the two best parents a boy could ever have. I can't back that up with statistics but I know in my heart that it's true.

Acknowledgments

The process of self publishing a book is largely a solitary activity but this project could not have been completed without the help of many others. Before I introduce the book, I would like to thank a few of those people for their contributions.

First, thanks to Samara Pearlstein for her cover design and numerous illustrations throughout the book. Her skilled art work helps to bring all of the formulas and numbers to life. Thanks also to Chuck Hildebrandt and Kurt Mensching for their very professional editing. Of course, if any errors managed to slip through after this process, they are solely my responsibility.

Thanks to all the individuals who helped review the manuscript at various stages of development. This includes Eddie Bajek, Sean Barrett, Benjamin Belcher, Mary Brolin, Eric Cioe, Gordon Fitzgerald, Jonathan Frankel, Howard Gould, Brandon Heipp, Justin Inaz, Mitchel Lichtman, Jeff Morford, Dave Nagi, Pete Palmer, Dave Studenmund, Tom Tango and Geoff Young.

Finally, thanks to all the Internet sites which provide volumes of data and analysis free of charge. This includes Baseball-Databank.org, BaseballMusings.com, Baseball-Reference.com, FanGraphs.com, HardballTimes.com and Retrosheet.org. These and many other sites will be cited throughout the book. A complete list can be found in the appendix.

Beyond Batting Average

Baseball Statistics for the 21st Century

Written by Lee Panas

Table of Contents

Introduction

When I first discovered the Internet in the early 1990s, I learned that it was a fascinating place for a baseball fan. I could visit message boards and talk to avid baseball fans from all over the country. I had access to live box scores of all games and up-to-date statistics for all players. I was able to follow the sport I love in ways not possible before. It was baseball heaven for a fantasy baseball team owner and a Detroit Tigers fan living in Massachusetts.

While the Internet provided a treasure of new baseball information and great conversations with serious fans, it became clear that the science of baseball statistics was not much more advanced in cyberspace than it was in the offline world. There were no sites such as BaseballProspectus.com, FanGraphs.com or HardballTimes.com where fans could read about new advances in baseball statistics. Blogs had not yet been conceived. Save for a few obscure forums here and there, there was little in the way of discussion of advanced data analysis.

Statistics as simple as on-base percentage and slugging average were rarely mentioned on popular baseball sites. Those who dared to evaluate players using measures beyond the usual batting average, home runs and runs batted in were told that they were making the game too complicated. Slowly but surely, though, more advanced metrics have made their way into the mainstream of the Internet. While the traditional fan is still in the majority, it is now hard to find an Internet baseball forum that does not have a good number of analysts peppering the discussion with modern metrics. In addition, dozens of statistics-themed sites and blogs are regularly pumping out new analyses, which would not have been dreamed of a decade earlier.

In the last few years, analytical discussion on the Internet has blossomed to the point where curiosity has become more common than resistance. However, the science of baseball is getting more and more complex and new information and methodologies are being developed at a rapid pace. People are more willing to learn about baseball statistics than ever before, but sometimes the information is coming too fast. The purpose of this book is to summarize many of the latest developments in baseball statistics for curious and intelligent fans, who like numbers but don't have time to figure it all out for themselves.

There are reasons why statistics are so popular among baseball fans. Baseball is the most individual of team sports and player performance is more easily and accurately measured in baseball than in any other sport. Statistics are also part of the reason why baseball has the most storied history of any team sport. We can go back in time and peruse the rosters and statistics of the 1927 Yankees or the 1975 Reds and immediately get a picture of the greatness of those teams. We can look at Lou Gehrig's career record and imagine what it would have been like to follow him on a regular basis.

In modern times, statistics have taken on a more important role. Since Bill James wrote his first *Baseball Abstract* in the late 1970s, there has been a data explosion in baseball. Statistics have become more complex and many fans have become more scientific in their interest in the national pastime. We have discovered that statistics are not only fun, but they can also lead to a greater understanding of how teams win ballgames.

The study of statistics in baseball even has a name – sabermetrics. Sabermetrics is the analysis of baseball through objective evidence, including statistics. The term was created by James who derived it from the acronym SABR, which stands for the Society for American Baseball Research, a popular organization devoted to baseball history.

In addition to fans, teams have also developed a stronger interest in sabermetrics in recent years. The Boston Red Sox, who won their first championship in 86 years under the sabermetric management of Theo Epstein, are one of the most prominent examples. The use of sabermetrics in baseball was first made widely known to fans in the book *Moneyball,* written by Michael Lewis in 2003. The book argued that Oakland Athletics General Manager Billy Beane was able to compete with wealthier teams by building a team based on empirical measures. Teams are now putting increased emphasis on data analysis in the management of their organizations.

This is not a book that describes how teams use statistics to manage their organizations. Rather, it is about how fans can use statistics to enhance their understanding of the game. In the last dozen years, I have spent countless hours on Internet baseball message boards and blogs engaging in debates about the game. What's the best way to build a team? Who should have been the American League MVP last year? Who is the best defensive third baseman in the game? Who is the most effective baserunner? These debates inevitably evolve into a discussion about statistics.

The book begins with a brief history of baseball statistics in Chapter 1. Some may be surprised to learn that the history of sabermetrics goes all the way back to the origins of the game in the 19th century. In chapter 2, we will dive into one of the central themes of sabermetrics, that is, how do teams win games? Very simply, they win games by scoring runs and preventing runs. In the remainder of the book, we will investigate how teams score runs and prevent runs and will learn how to determine which players contribute the most to their teams in terms of runs scored and runs prevented.

Starting with chapter 3, we will systematically break down all the elements of the game – hitting, baserunning, pitching and fielding – and describe them from a statistical perspective. Chapters 3 through 6 cover batting statistics. Chapter 7 discusses baserunning. Chapters 8 through 10 review pitching. Chapters 11 through 13 delve into fielding. Chapter 14 explores methods for comparing players who played in different contexts, including ballparks, leagues and eras. Finally, Chapter 15 combines all the information of the previous chapters into statistics that estimate player value in terms of wins.

While this book requires little prior knowledge of modern statistical analysis, I have assumed that the reader will be very knowledgeable about baseball and has an interest in looking at new ways to answer questions about the game. You may be a high school baseball coach who knows all the nuts and bolts of the game on the field but is learning about new baseball statistics for the first time and wants to know what they are all about. Or, you may be a mathematics or engineering student who loves numbers, logic and analysis and wants to apply them to your favorite sport. Maybe you are a just an ordinary fan who walked into an Internet debate and saw people talking about zone rating or runs created and you want to learn more about those kinds of topics.

With the Internet today, you can go to a search engine such as Google and type "zone rating" and you'll get some kind of explanation. If you go to enough different links you'll find one that you'll understand. That can be frustrating though because it can take time to find what you want and it takes even longer to find out how the statistic you are looking up fits with all the other measures. This book puts everything in one place for you. It also includes many examples which tie the statistics together and show how they can be used to evaluate players and teams.

My goal is to explain the new world of baseball statistics in a way that any knowledgeable and curious baseball fan will comprehend. At the very least, I anticipate that it will make readers understand the debates better. It is also my desire that it will help analysts themselves explain concepts better to people when they bring them into discussion. Most of all, my hope is that the book will enhance the reader's enjoyment and understanding of the game.

Chapter 1

History of Baseball Statistics

There is a common misconception that statistical analysis and debate in baseball began with Bill James in the late 1970s. In fact, baseball has a long fascinating history of statistics going back to the origins of the game in the 19th Century. An excellent account of the evolution of baseball statistics was given in *The Numbers Game,* written by Alan Schwarz in 2004. The history of the game's quantification is also covered in an early chapter of *The Hidden Game of Baseball,* written by John Thorn and Pete Palmer in 1984. A brief summary of the history of baseball statistics is presented here.

EARLY BOX SCORES

Shortly after Alexander Cartwright and the New York Knickerbockers established the first set of modern baseball rules, the first box score appeared in the *New York Morning News* on October 25, 1845, and was reprinted in *The Hidden Game of Baseball* (See Figure 1 below). The only statistics that were included in this box score were hands out (Today, they are simply called "outs".) and runs for batters. Some of the early baseball writers had ties to cricket, a relative of baseball, and early box scores reflected that association. Hits that did not result in runs were not included because, in cricket, one either scores a point by reaching the opposite wicket or is out.

Figure 1: The First Box Score, October 25, 1845

NEW YORK BALL CLUB			BROOKLYN CLUB		
	Hands out	**Runs**		**Hands out**	**Runs**
Davis	2	4	Hunt	1	3
Murphy	0	6	Hines	2	2
Vail	2	4	Gilmore	3	2
Kline	1	4	Hardy	2	2
Miller	2	5	Sharp	2	2
Case	2	4	Meyers	0	3
Tucker	2	4	Whaley	2	2
Winslow	1	6	Forman	1	3
	12	**37**		**12***	**19**

*The Hands out total was 13 but was erroneously typed in the New York Morning News as 12.

Source: The Hidden Game of Baseball, Pg. 11

Surprisingly, some early box scores were quite detailed. Figure 2 shows a partial box score of an all-star game that originally appeared in the *New York Tribune* in 1858 and was reprinted in *The*

Hidden Game of Baseball. It included the following statistics for batters: outs, runs and times put out on flies, bounds (Balls caught on one bounce were outs at that time.) and foul balls. Pitchers were not allowed to snap their wrists and did not try to retire batters, but were to instead let the batters put the ball in play. Thus, no pitching statistics were included in early box scores, but fielding was covered in more detail than it is in today's box scores. Statistics provided were fly balls caught, balls caught on bound and times putting out runners on base. For baserunners, the 1858 box score included: how often put out at first, second and third.

Figure 2: Portion of Box Score of 1858 All-Star Game

| | Outs | Runs | BROOKLYN FIELDING | | | | HOW PUT OUT | | | | | |
			Fly	Bound	Base	Total	Fly	Bound	1b	2b	3b	Foul
Leggett, c	5	1	0	7	0	7	1	1	1	0	0	2
Holder, 2b	4	2	0	0	1	1	1	1	0	0	0	2
Pidgeon, ss	4	1	2	2	1	5	1	0	1	1	0	1
Grum, cf	2	4	0	0	0	0	1	0	0	0	0	1
P. O'Brien, lf	3	2	0	3	0	3	1	0	0	1	0	1
Price, 1b	1	3	0	0	4	4	0	0	0	1	0	0
M. O'Brien, p	2	3	2	1	1	4	0	1	0	0	0	1
Masten, 3b	4	1	2	1	0	3	1	2	1	0	0	0
Burr, rf	2	1	0	0	0	0	0	1	1	0	0	0
	27	**18**	**6**	**14**	**7**	**27**	**6**	**6**	**4**	**3**	**0**	**8**

Source: The Hidden Game of Baseball, Pg. 13

CUMULATIVE TRACKING OF STATISTICS

The next step after the development of box scores was to combine data from individual games to get summary statistics for entire seasons. The first person known to track baseball statistics cumulatively was Henry Chadwick. Born in 1824 in England, Chadwick was a writer, a cricket aficionado and baseball's first statistician. Chadwick, who is considered by some historians to be the "father of baseball", spent the latter half of the century designing box scores, developing new statistics and otherwise defining the new game. He kept track of cumulative statistics which could be used to assess players' performance and reported them in the *New York Clipper, Beadle Dime Base-Ball Player* (*Beadle Guide*) and other publications. The 1861 *Beadle Guide* included the following totals for players on five teams: Games, outs, runs, homers and strike outs for batters. Hits, however, were left out.

EVOLUTION OF BATTING STATISTICS

Noticing that cumulative statistics were dependent on playing time and that not all teams played the same number of games, Chadwick introduced runs per game and outs per game in the 1865 *Clipper.* Twenty-two years after the first known box score, Chadwick introduced the hit in 1867 in the *Ball Players' Chronicle*, a weekly baseball publication. He also included hits per game, total bases, total bases per game and home runs. Soon, hits per game and total bases per game replaced runs per game as the most popular batting statistics.

In 1872, H.A. Dobson, a fan from Washington, wrote to Chadwick arguing that hits per game and total bases per game favored leadoff hitters who batted more often than hitters lower in the order. Dobson suggested a new statistic: hits (H) per time at bat (AB), which became known as batting average (BA) shortly thereafter. Chadwick included batting average in the 1872 *Beadle guide* and declared it to be the best measure of hitting performance. It was adopted as an official statistic by the National League in 1876. Figure 3 shows the National League batting average leaders that year.

Figure 3: National League Batting Average Leaders, 1876

Player	Team	AB	H	BA
Ross Barnes	Chicago	322	138	.429
George Hall	Philadelphia	268	98	.366
Cap Anson	Chicago	309	110	.356

Source: Baseball-Reference.com

Just as many do today, 19th century fans protested that batting average did not take total bases and bases on balls (BB) into account. However, Chadwick was not impressed by the power game and did not emphasize home runs, total bases or home runs per game. Thus, batting average became the most widely used statistic and it remained the measure of choice of baseball insiders and fans for a long time. Because power hitting was not highly regarded, slugging average did not become an official statistic until 1923 in the National League and 1946 in the American League. Additionally, bases on balls did not become an official statistic until 1910 in the National League and 1913 in the American League

In 1879, the National League tracked "times reached first base" but this forerunner of on-base percentage was eliminated after one year. In 1887, the National League and American Association added walks to batting average as if they were hits but that practice also lasted for only one year. Figure 4 lists the American Association batting average leaders in 1887. It includes their batting average as computed in 1887 as well as their traditional batting average calculated without walks. No such statistic was again promoted publicly until statistician Allan Roth introduced on-base percentage to long time Major League Baseball (MLB) executive Branch Rickey in the early 1950s. On-base percentage did not become an official statistic until 1984.

Figure 4: American Association Batting Average Leaders, 1887

Player	Team	AB	H	BB	1887 BA	Traditional BA
Tip O'Neill	St. Louis	517	225	50	.485	.435
Pete Browning	Louisville	547	220	55	.457	.402
Dave Orr	New York	345	127	22	.406	.368

Source: Baseball-Reference.com

Similar to walks and slugging average, it took a long time for runs batted in to become a permanent fixture. The runs batted in statistic was recorded in newspapers in 1879 and 1880 and was an official statistic in the National League in 1891. However, fans complained that the measure was unfair to leadoff batters and too dependent on opportunity and it was quickly dropped. Ernie Lanigan, an important baseball statistician in the early 20th century, personally tracked runs batted in and included the statistic in *New York Press* box scores starting in 1907. It became an official statistic again in 1920 under the name, "Runs Responsible For".

As pitching became stronger near the end of the century, "small ball" measures became popular. The stolen base was first recorded in 1886 but was defined differently than it is today: a player was credited with a stolen base when he advanced an extra base on a hit (e.g. went from first to third on a single). The modern definition of the stolen base came into being in 1898. Sacrifice bunts were first recorded in 1889 to encourage and reward team play. By 1893, they were no longer counted as at bats.

EVOLUTION OF PITCHING STATISTICS

In 1872, the rule against the pitcher wrist snap was dropped and pitchers became an important part of the game. By 1876, there were eleven official pitching categories including earned runs per game, hits allowed, hits per game and batting average against. Strikeouts were not included initially because Chadwick saw them as a sign of poor batting rather than good pitching. Strikeouts did not become an official pitching statistic until 1887. Pitcher win/loss records were first tracked in the mid 1880s.

With relief pitching becoming more prominent, *The Reach Guide* published the statistic "Times Taken Out" in 1905. This measure is the opposite of today's complete games. In 1912, National League president John Heydler dropped earned runs per game and added earned runs per nine innings pitched, which is now known as earned run average. At the time, win/loss records for pitchers were also dropped from the official statistics, but they returned in 1920. In Chapter 8, we will discuss why the win/loss statistic is a questionable measure of individual performance, especially in today's game.

Given the ever changing role of relief pitchers and the knowledge that wins/losses and ERA were not sufficient for describing reliever performance, the save statistic was developed by Chicago Sun-Times writer Jerome Holtzman in 1960. Originally, a pitcher was given credit for a save when he came into a game with the tying or winning run on base or at plate and finished the game. The measure evolved over time and became an official statistic in 1969. Relief pitching statistics will be discussed in detail in Chapter 10.

EVOLUTION OF FIELDING STATISTICS

Fielding statistics evolved more slowly than batting and pitching statistics. In 1863, catches missed (now called errors) were first recorded and appeared in the *New York Sunday Mercury*. Four years later, Chadwick made the distinction between earned and unearned runs – not for pitchers but for fielders and batters. Fielders were evaluated based on putouts, assists and errors. When the National League was formed in 1876, its official fielding measure was fielding percentage (Chapter 11) and it remained the primary official defensive statistic for more than one hundred years.

In 1872, Philadelphia Athletics scorer Mr. Reed started rating fielders by average putouts per game, average outs per game and chances per game. Realizing that plays made were more important than errors avoided, Chadwick supported Reed's practice and added these statistics in his 1872 *Beadle Guide*. These concepts were largely unrecognized, however, until James introduced the range factor statistic more than one hundred years later. Range factor and other more advanced fielding measures will be covered in Chapters 11-13.

EARLY SABERMETRICIANS

More complex measures, which comprise the bulk of this book, also have a long history. Ferdinand Cole Lane, former biologist and editor of the *Baseball Magazine* from 1910-1937, often wrote about the limitations of statistics. Among other things, Lane rallied against batting average bemoaning the fact that it ignored both walks and extra base hits. He opposed pitcher won-loss records and fielding percentage and talked about the importance of ballpark factors. Lane also collected play-by-play data over many games to determine the run impact of singles, doubles, triples and homers, and determined that slugging average did not weight the hits properly. Lane was a man before his time, though, and most of his ideas did not become popular until decades later.

When he was hired by Rickey in 1947, Roth became baseball's first full-time team statistician. Among other things, he developed a complicated formula which boiled every aspect of baseball into one number. Two parts of the formula were on-base percentage and isolated power, statistics that will be covered in detail in Chapter 3. Rickey, the first known sabermetric general manager, used these statistics in player evaluation and wrote about them in a 1954 *Life Magazine* article entitled "GoodBy to Some Old Baseball Ideas". However, this concept of combining multiple player skills into a single number would not become widely fashionable until many years later.

George Lindsey, a military strategist by trade, applied his skills to baseball in the mid 1950s. After tracking hundreds of games in detail, as Cole did earlier, Lindsey developed a run expectation matrix – a tabulation of expected runs in any situation depending on outs and runners on base. This allowed him to assess the strategic value of stolen bases, sacrifice bunts and other events. Lindsey also confirmed Cole's earlier conclusion that different types of hits were not being valued properly. Unfortunately, Lindsey's work appeared only in obscure journals and was largely ignored

Unaware of Lindsey's research, retired engineer Earnshaw Cook started from scratch and reached some of the same conclusions, which he published in *Percentage Baseball* in 1964. Critics said that the book was too complex for the average fan and mathematicians felt that it was sloppy statistically, but it was still an important piece in the development of sabermetrics. While Cook's overall influence of the game was small, he did reach some young mathematically minded fans, such as Palmer, and even caught the attention of long-time player and manager Dave Johnson. The work of Cole, Lindsey, Cook and Palmer will be discussed further in Chapter 5.

BILL JAMES

The first analyst to deliver sabermetrics to the masses was Bill James. James answered questions about baseball in the *Baseball Abstract,* published annually from 1977-1988, and became quite popular, in part, because of his witty writing style. He was profiled in *Sports Illustrated* in an article entitled "He Does It by the Numbers," written by Dan Okrent in 1981. Shortly thereafter, the *Baseball Abstract* became a best seller. The mainstream media avoided sabermetrics for the most part, but advanced statistical analysis of baseball had finally reached a sizable audience. Many others have followed, but James is considered by many to be the godfather of sabermetrics. He was hired as a statistical consultant by the Boston Red Sox in 2003.

EARL WEAVER

During his tenure as manager of the Baltimore Orioles from 1968-1982 and 1985-1986, Earl Weaver was one of the first managers known to rely heavily on statistics. Whereas most managers of the period depended largely on observation and instinct, Weaver gathered as much data on players as he could find and used them in his decision making. For example, rather than relying on memory, he personally kept track of how batters fared against each pitcher. From that point, managers and front offices gradually began to make more use of statistics, and fans became hungry for new statistical information as well.

MONEYBALL

When Michael Lewis wrote the book *Moneyball* in 2003, a whole new group of fans became part of the sabermetric explosion. *Moneyball* revealed Oakland Athletics General Manager Billy Beane's analytical approach to building a baseball team with a small budget. One of the themes of the book was that the wisdom of some baseball insiders (including players, managers, coaches, scouts and general managers) was too subjective and often flawed. The book argued that the Athletics were able to compete with wealthier teams by building a team based on undervalued empirical measures.

WRAP-UP

More and more statisticians are being introduced to the game and the role of sabermetrics in the decision making of major league teams is growing each year. For this reason, it makes sense for fans to gain a better understanding of some of the more advanced statistical methodologies used in modern baseball. In the remaining chapters, we look at many of the new measures that have been developed in recent years and discuss why they may be more useful in player evaluation, projection and team building than the traditional numbers.

Illustration by Samara Pearlstein

Chapter 2

Winning Games

A contributor to the Detroit Tigers fan forum MotownSports.com once said: "I'm a bottom line guy. The only statistics that matter to me are wins and losses." In the end, wins and losses are indeed what matter, so let's start there. How do teams win games? The simple answer is that they need to outscore their opponents, so those teams with the most runs scored and the fewest runs allowed over the course of a season should win the most games. Some will argue that it's not how many runs a team scores but when they score them that counts. By this, they mean that good teams might not outscore their opponents by much, but they win because of effective situational or clutch hitting and pitching.

WINS VERSUS RUN DIFFERENTIAL

Figure 5 shows us the relationship between wins (W) and run differential (Run Diff), that is, runs scored minus runs allowed, for National League teams in 2008. For example, the Chicago Cubs scored 855 runs and allowed 671 runs yielding a run differential of +184 (855-671). Similarly, the San Francisco Giants had a run differential of -119 (640-759).

Figure 5: Wins vs. Run Differential for National League Teams, 2008

Team	W	Run Diff
Chicago	97	184
Philadelphia	92	119
Milwaukee	90	61
New York	89	84
Houston	86	-31
St. Louis	86	54
Florida	84	3
Los Angeles	84	52
Arizona	82	14
Cincinnati	74	-96
Colorado	74	-75
Atlanta	72	-25
San Francisco	72	-119
Pittsburgh	67	-149
San Diego	63	-127
Washington	59	-184

Data from Baseball-Reference.com

Figure 5 reveals that the top four run differentials went to the four teams with the most wins. The bottom four run differentials belonged to the teams with the four lowest win totals. While there were a couple of exceptions, it appears as if winning was largely a function of the obvious – scoring more runs and allowing fewer runs.

Pete Palmer estimated that a differential of ten runs is worth approximately one win. In other words, adding ten runs to a team's season total increases their expected wins (EW) by one and subtracting ten runs decreases their expected wins by one. Palmer developed the following formula for expected wins (EW) based on that principle:

$$EW = games/2 + (Run\ Diff)/10$$

According to their +184 run differential, the Cubs had $81 + 184/10 = 99$ expected wins. That was just two more that their actual number of wins, so Palmer's formula closely models reality in the case of the Cubs. The same calculation for the Padres (-127 run differential) yielded $81 - 127/10 = 68$ expected wins, which was five more than their actual number of wins. Figure 6 shows the actual wins, expected wins based on Palmer's formula, and the difference between the two (W-EW) for all National League teams in 2008.

Figure 6: Wins vs. Expected Wins for National League Teams, 2008

Team	W	EW	W-EW
Chicago	97	99	-2
Philadelphia	92	93	-1
Milwaukee	90	87	+3
New York	89	89	0
Houston	86	77	+9
St. Louis	86	86	0
Florida	84	81	+3
Los Angeles	84	86	-2
Arizona	82	82	0
Cincinnati	74	71	+3
Colorado	74	73	+1
Atlanta	72	79	-7
San Francisco	72	69	+3
Pittsburgh	67	66	+1
San Diego	63	68	-5
Washington	59	62	-3

Data from Baseball-Reference.com

The expected win totals were pretty close to the actual win totals in most cases, with all but two teams coming within five wins. The two teams were the Houston Astros who exceeded their estimate by nine wins and the Atlanta Braves who undershot their predicted total by seven wins.

When a team performs far above its expected wins, as the Astros did, it usually means that they either did very well in close games or they lost a disproportionate number of games by wide margins. Data from BaseballProspectus.com reveals that the Astros outperformed by nine wins thanks, in part, to a 2-10 record in games decided by eight or more runs.

Conversely, teams such as the Braves, who fell significantly short of their expected wins, usually did so because they did poorly in close games or won a large number of games where they substantially outscored their opponents. According to BaseballProspectus.com, the Braves underperformed their expected wins by seven wins partly because of their 11-30 record in one-run games.

The run differential formula works reasonably well in most years for most teams. From 1988-2008 (excluding the strike year of 1994), about 85% of MLB teams came within five wins of their expected wins. That means that an average of two teams in each league each year fell outside that range.

PYTHAGOREAN THEOREM

A more popular model of the relationship between a team's runs scored (RS), runs allowed (RA) and wins is the Pythagorean Theorem introduced by Bill James in his 1980 *Baseball Abstract.* That may sound like something you heard about in a high school geometry class, but it is not complicated. It is calculated as follows:

$$\text{Pythagorean percentage} = (RS^2)/(RS^2 + RA^2)$$

For example, the Cubs scored 855 runs and allowed 671 runs in 2008. Plugging those numbers into the above formula yields

$$\text{Pythagorean percentage} = (855 \times 855)/(855 \times 855 + 671 \times 671) = .619$$

Chicago's .619 Pythagorean percentage translates into 100 predicted wins over a full season, which is just three more than their actual number of wins.

Looking at teams from 1919-2008, the Pythagorean Theorem and the run differential method described above predict wins from runs scored and runs allowed with very similar precision. Both methods lose some accuracy when used to calculate expected wins in the lower run-scoring Deadball Era from 1901-1918, when a run was worth more in terms of wins, than it is in a higher run-scoring environment.

The Pythagorean Theorem has been tweaked over time and it has been found empirically that the optimal exponent to use in the formula is 1.83 instead of 2. While an exponent of 2 is sufficient for most practical purposes, some may wish to use 1.83 when more precision is desired.

WINS, EXPECTED WINS AND RELIEF PITCHING

Beyond records in close games and blow outs, what kinds of teams tend to stray from their expected win estimates using either of the methods presented above? Baseball Prospectus co-founder Rany Jazayerli and former Baseball Prospectus writer and current researcher for an MLB team Keith Woolner studied the relationship between bullpens and the Pythagorean Theorem. In their work published at ESPN.com in 1999, they compared the teams with the 102 best and worst relief staffs from 1980-1998 (excluding the strike shortened 1981 and 1994 seasons) based on various statistics. They discovered that teams with the strongest bullpens won

1.3 more games on average than they should have based on the Pythagorean Theorem. Conversely, teams with relatively weak bullpens won 1.6 fewer games than expected.

Jazayerli and Woolner also discovered that teams with good bullpens tended to exceed their expected record in one-run games while teams with poor bullpens were more likely to underperform in one-run games. Their study does not explain all of the discrepancies between actual and expected win totals but bullpen quality is the biggest factor that has been found to date.

OFFENSE VERSUS DEFENSE

While we have discussed some exceptions, we have seen that runs scored and runs allowed are fairly highly correlated with winning percentage. But isn't defense more important than offense? We've heard that "good pitching beats good hitting all of the time." We've also been told that "pitching and fielding win pennants" and that "pitching is 75% of the game."

To test those theories, I examined the relative importance of offense and defense (pitching/fielding combined) in reaching the playoffs for all postseason participants from 1988-2008. I ranked each team in every year based on offense (runs scored) and defense (runs allowed). Then, each team's offense was ranked as "Good", "OK" or "Poor" based on their rank. If a team finished in the top third of the league in runs scored, then it was considered Good. If it finished in the middle third, then it was placed into the OK group. Teams in the bottom third were classified as Poor. Team defense was categorized the same way (Good, OK, Poor) based on runs allowed.

Crossing the offense classification (Good, OK, Poor) with the defense classification (Good, OK, Poor) yielded nine categories (Good offense and Good defense, OK offense and Good defense, etc) shown in Figure 7. For example, the 2008 Brewers were seventh in the National League in runs scored and had the fourth fewest runs allowed, so they went into the OK offense/Good defense category.

Figure 7: Offense and Defense of Playoff teams, 1988-2008

Offense	Defense	No.	%
Good	Good	49	36
OK	Good	37	27
Good	OK	26	19
OK	OK	8	6
Poor	Good	8	6
Good	Poor	6	4
Poor	OK	2	2
OK	Poor	0	0
Poor	Poor	0	0

Data from Baseball-Databank.org

Of the 136 playoff teams from 1988-2008, 49 were categorized as Good offense/Good defense. The next most frequent categories were OK offense/ Good defense (37) followed by Good offense/ OK defense (26). Other combinations were less common.

What can we conclude from these data? More than one-third (36%) of the teams that made the playoffs had both strong offense and defense, so it is important for an organization to try to build both components. Additionally, it was a little more common for an OK offense/Good defense team to make the playoffs than a Good offense/OK defense team, but it was not that much more common. This tells us that there is more than one way to build a team for postseason and that dominant pitching and defense are not always essential. What about teams with Poor offense/Good defense or Good offense/Poor defense? The low numbers in those categories (eight and six respectively) tell us that neither is a particularly good way to build a team, but one is not worse than the other.

I also researched earlier eras starting with the Deadball Era to see if the same patterns revealed for 1988-2008 held since the beginning of postseason play. I found that the only real difference between time periods was related to the percentage of teams that made the postseason. With a smaller percentage of teams making the playoffs prior to divisional play in 1969 and expanded playoffs in 1995, there were a greater proportion of teams in the Good offense/ Good defense category in the earlier years. However, there was no era where either offense or defense was substantially more important than the other.

WRAP-UP

We learned in this chapter that winning games is fairly tightly tied to the number of runs scored and allowed by teams. We also discovered that quality defense is only slightly more important than quality offense in building teams for postseason and that the typical playoff team is strong in both areas. In the remaining chapters of the book, we will see how teams score runs and prevent runs and explore ways to determine which players produced and prevented the most runs for their teams.

llustration by Samara Pearlstein

Chapter 3

Basic Batting

The Chicago White Sox had a low team batting average in 2008, but finished among the top five in the American League in runs scored by blasting a league-leading 235 home runs. The Boston Red Sox had 62 fewer homers than the Pale Hose but outscored them by hitting for average, drawing walks and slugging doubles. The Minnesota Twins did not hit for much power nor draw many walks, but finished third in the league in runs on the strength of singles, baserunning and timely hitting. What matters for an offense is that it produces as many runs as possible whatever way this is accomplished. One of the most important areas of sabermetrics is the determination of run contribution by players to their teams. This is the topic of Chapters 3-6.

HOW RUNS ARE SCORED

In Chapter 2, we confirmed the importance of run scoring in winning games. The next question is: How does a team score runs? Most simply, a team scores runs by stringing together the following events while avoiding outs:

1. Singles (1B)
2. Doubles (2B)
3. Triples (3B)
4. Home runs (HR)
5. Bases on balls (BB) including intentional bases on balls (IBB)
6. Hit batsmen (HBP)
7. Reaching base on errors (ROE)
8. Sacrifice bunts (SH)
9. Sacrifice flies (SF)
10. Stolen bases (SB)
11. Other baserunning plays

We'll concentrate on the first six items for now as those events are easily measured and account for most of run scoring. The ROE, SH and SF events occur relatively infrequently and pale in comparison to hits and walks in terms of the information they provide about run scoring. For those interested in a detailed discussion of the utility of sacrifice bunting, I suggest consulting *The Book – Playing the Percentages in Baseball,* written by Tom Tango, Mitchel Lichtman and Andrew Dolphin in 2006. Baserunning is a significant portion of offense but it is more difficult to measure and will be covered in Chapter 7 of this book.

The offenses of the 2008 Texas Rangers and Oakland Athletics are compared in Figure 8 below. Since the Rangers topped the Athletics in all six categories (1B, 2B, 3B, HR, BB, HBP), most would guess that they scored more runs than Oakland, and they would be correct. The Rangers scored 901 runs and the Athletics scored 646.

Figure 8: Batting Lines for Texas Rangers and Oakland Athletics, 2008

Team	1B	2B	3B	HR	BB	HBP
Texas	1014	376	35	194	595	63
Oakland	900	270	23	125	574	48

Source: Baseball-Reference.com

The same statistics that are used to assess teams can also be used to evaluate players. Figure 9 compares the 2008 seasons of Philadelphia Phillies second baseman Chase Utley and Atlanta Braves outfielder Jeff Francouer. In about the same amount of playing time, Utley led Francouer in all six offensive categories. Any knowledgeable fan would conclude from these data that Utley had a better offensive season than Francouer.

Figure 9: Chase Utley vs. Jeff Francouer, 2008

Player	AB	1B	2B	3B	HR	BB	HBP
Chase Utley	607	99	41	4	33	64	27
Jeff Francouer	599	96	33	3	11	39	10

Source: Baseball-Reference.com

People sometimes ask why it is necessary to combine these simple statistics into more complicated measures when we can just look at the raw data and determine whether a hitter had a good season. It's true that looking at an entire line of data is ideal in making comparisons between two players, but suppose we want to determine the best ten hitters in the past five years or even one year. We could try to eyeball all of the different statistical lines, but it would be pretty difficult to keep track of everything for such a large number of players. Thus, it's valuable to have ways to combine the raw statistics in ways that help us answer broader questions.

Many of the most popular combination statistics depend on plate appearances (PA) and at bats (AB). A batter is charged with a PA every time he comes to bat with two exceptions: (1) a baserunner is thrown out stealing or picked off to end an inning while that batter is still at the plate or (2) the batter is replaced in the middle of an at bat by a pinch hitter. In that case, the pinch hitter will get the PA, unless there are two strikes when he comes to bat and the pitcher records a strikeout. In that instance, the original batter gets the PA and the strikeout. At bats count all PA excluding BB, HBP, SF and SH:

$$AB = PA - (BB + HBP + SF + SH)$$

BATTING AVERAGE

The most popular statistic among many fans and media has long been batting average. Batting average (BA or AVG) is the proportion of at bats that result in hits. For example, Utley had the following statistics in 2008:

$$AB = 607$$

$$H = 177$$

$$BA = H/AB = 177/607 = .292$$

Fans know that a .300 BA is good, a .220 BA is bad and that a .400 BA is both fantastic and rare. Despite its reputation in some quarters of the statistical community, batting average is not an awful statistic. The ability to make good contact and to hit the ball where fielders can't get to it is a positive attribute. It's also true that teams that hit for a high batting average tend to score large numbers of runs.

Figure 10 shows the relationship between batting average and runs scored for MLB teams in 2008. Teams with higher batting averages tended to score more runs than teams with lower batting averages, but there was a good deal of variation. The Royals batted .269 (9th in MLB) but only scored 691 runs (25th). Conversely, the White Sox batted .263 (16th) but scored 811 runs (6th). So, it's clear that batting average does not always work well by itself in describing a team's offensive output.

Figure 10: Runs vs. Batting Average for MLB Teams, 2008

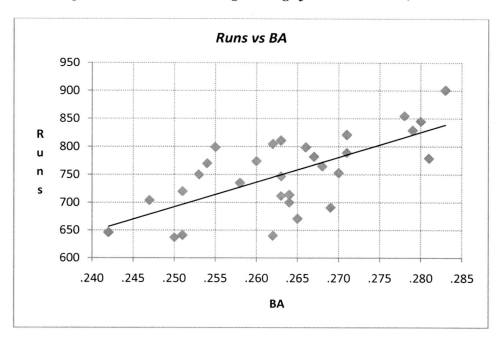

Data from Baseball-Databank.org

ON-BASE PERCENTAGE

Most fans realize intuitively that BA has shortcomings but it becomes more obvious when we look at an example. The 2006 seasons for Detroit Tigers catcher Ivan Rodriguez and New York Yankees first baseman Jason Giambi are displayed in Figure 11.

Figure 11: Ivan Rodriguez vs. Jason Giambi, 2006

Player	AB	H	2B	3B	HR	BB	HBP	SF	BA
Ivan Rodriguez	547	164	28	4	13	26	1	2	.300
Jason Giambi	446	113	25	0	37	110	16	7	.253

Source: Baseball-Reference.com

Which one had the better offensive season? Rodriguez clearly had the higher BA (.300 versus .253) but Giambi had many more HR, BB and HBP. So, BA by itself isn't going to answer the question here. To take hits and walks into account, we can calculate times on base (TOB) and then on-base percentage (OBP). OBP is the proportion of plate appearances (minus SH) in which a batter reached base on a hit, walk or hit batsman:

$$TOB = (H + BB + HBP)$$

$$OBP = TOB/ (AB + BB + HBP + SF)$$

The OBP calculations for Rodriguez and Giambi are displayed below:

Rodriguez: OBP = (164 + 26 + 1)/ (547 + 26 + 1 + 2) = .332

Giambi: OBP = (113 + 110 + 16)/ (446 + 110 + 16 + 7) =.413

While Rodriguez had the higher BA by 0.047, Giambi had the superior OBP by 0.081. This means that Giambi was on base 24% more often than Rodriguez.

SLUGGING AVERAGE

Another limitation of BA is that it counts all hits equally even though some hits (e.g. homers) are clearly worth more than others (e.g. singles). Slugging Average (SLG) is based on total bases (TB) for the batter. The TB statistic is calculated by weighting hits according to how many bases the batter gained – one for a single (1B), two for a double (2B), three for a triple (3B) and four for a home run (HR):

$$TB = 1B + 2 \times 2B + 3 \times 3B + 4 \times HR$$

The slugging average statistic measures TB per AB. It is often called slugging percentage but that is a misnomer, as it is really an average. If someone has a SLG of .500, it does not mean that he did something in half of his at bats as a percentage or proportion would suggest. It means that he averaged 0.5 bases per at bat. The formula for SLG is:

$$SLG = TB/AB$$

The slugging averages for Rodriguez and Giambi can be easily computed from their 2006 statistics:

<u>Rodriguez</u>

TB = 119 + 2 x 28 + 3 x 4 + 4 x 13 = 239

AB = 547

SLG = TB/AB = 239/547 = .437

<u>Giambi</u>

TB = 249

AB = 446

SLG = 249/446 = .558

Not only did Giambi get on base at a higher rate than Rodriguez, but he was also superior to Rodriguez in slugging by .121. In other words, Giambi got one extra base over Rodriguez in every eight at bats.

BA/OBP/SLG LINE

The most popular batting summary given to describe a player has long been BA/HR/RBI. We have already covered the limitations of BA and we will discuss some of the concerns about HR and RBI shortly. Another statistical line that has become common, especially on the Internet is BA/OBP/SLG. For example, Rodriguez batted .300/.332/.437 and Giambi batted .253/.413/.558 in 2006. This statistical trio provides a good summary of offensive production combining the ability to hit for average, to get on base and to hit for power.

EXTRA-ON-BASE PERCENTAGE

One criticism of OBP and SLG is that neither really measures a specific batting skill. OBP combines hitting for average with getting on base without a hit, two events which involve different talents. Similarly, SLG combines hitting for average with hitting for extra bases or power, results which also entail two distinct abilities. Ideally, we would like to find statistics that measure three hitting skills separately: hitting for average, getting on base without a hit (which is mostly drawing walks) and hitting for power.

Figure 12 shows that Philadelphia Phillies outfielder Pat Burrell and Colorado Rockies slugger Matt Holliday had very similar OBPs in 2007 but they were different types of hitters. Whereas Burrell relied on drawing walks to get on base, Holliday depended more on hitting for average.

Figure 12: Pat Burrell vs. Matt Holliday, 2007

Player	PA	BA	OBP	BB	HBP
Pat Burrell	598	.256	.400	114	4
Matt Holliday	713	.340	.405	63	10

Source: Baseball-Reference.com

We can extract BB and HBP from the OBP calculation to look at a player's on-base contribution beyond hits. The sum of BB and HBP can then be divided by PA to arrive at a statistic I call extra-on-base percentage (EOBP). EOBP represents the portion of OBP not accounted for by BA. Burrell's 2007 EOBP is simple to calculate:

$$PA = 598$$

$$BB = 114$$

$$HBP = 4$$

$$EOBP = (BB + HBP)/PA = (114 + 4)/598 = .197$$

Burrell's .197 EOBP was 95 points higher than Holliday's .102 EOBP. EOBP is not tracked on a regular basis, but base on balls percentage (BB%) – percentage of PA which result in walks – can be found at FanGraphs.com. Since most batters are not often hit by pitches, BB% is usually similar to EOBP.

ISOLATED POWER

How can we best measure power? Home run totals (or even at bats per home run) are limited because they do not take doubles and triples into account. Slugging average adds doubles and triples into the equation but it also includes singles which generally do not involve power. Another statistic, isolated power (ISO), was developed by Branch Rickey and Allan Roth in the 1950s and was re-introduced by Bill James in 1977. ISO defines a hitter's ability to get extra bases on hits by separating doubles, triples and home runs from singles. It is the number of extra bases per at bat:

$$ISO = (2B + 2 \times 3B + 3 \times HR)/AB$$

ISO can also be calculated by subtracting BA from SLG:

$$ISO = SLG - BA$$

Figure 13 compares the statistics of outfielders Vladimir Guerrero of the Los Angeles Angels and Jack Cust of the Oakland Athletics in 2007. Guerrero had a higher SLG than Cust (.547 versus .504) but much of his advantage was due to singles rather than power. Most of Cust's SLG came from extra base hits and, as a result, Cust topped Guerrero in ISO .248 to .223. This tells us that, while Guerrero was the better hitter overall, Cust hit for more power. ISO is also tracked at FanGraphs.com.

Figure 13: Vladimir Guerrero vs. Jack Cust, 2007

Player	BA	OBP	SLG	ISO
Vladimir Guerrero	.324	.403	.547	.223
Jack Cust	.256	.408	.504	.248

Source: FanGraphs.com

A NEW BATTING LINE: BA/EOBP/ISO

The new statistics introduced above give us the batting line BA/EOBP/ISO (or BA/BB%/ISO) that differentiates the specific batting skills better than BA/OBP/SLG. BA loosely describes contact hitting; EOBP says something about batting eye; and ISO measures power. My rule of thumb is that a batter who is above average on two of these three skills will generally be a productive batter.

The BA/EOBP/ISO trio can be used to determine the most well rounded hitters in the game. Figure 14 lists the four players with regular playing time (400 or more PA) in the American League in 2008 finishing in the top 30 percent in all three hitting categories. This group had the most complete package of batting skills – hitting for average, drawing walks and hitting for power – in the league.

Figure 14: Best All Around Hitters in American League, 2008

Player	PA	BA	EOBP	ISO
Alex Rodriguez	594	.302	.133	.271
Milton Bradley	510	.321	.175	.242
Kevin Youkilis	621	.312	.119	.257
Manny Ramirez	425	.299	.141	.230

Data from Baseball-Databank.org

Both the BA/OBP/SLG and BA/EOBP/ISO combinations are limited, due to the fact that they fail to take playing time into account. For example, a hitter with a .300 BA/.360 OBP/.500 SLG in 600 PA would contribute more to his team than a hitter with the same line in 300 PA. David Bloom, of BaseballHappenings.com, suggests using OBP/SLG/TOB/TB because it combines both rate measures (OBP, SLG) and playing time statistics (TOB, TB). However, BA/OBP/SLG is still the most common combination in the sabermetric community.

PERCENTILES

Figure 15 shows the percentiles for some of the statistics presented in this chapter. For example, the 75th percentile for BA for MLB regulars or semi-regulars with 400 or more PA in 2008 was .293. This means that 75 percent of these players hit below .293 and 25 percent hit better than that. This chart should help those who are unfamiliar with some of the less common statistics to grasp them a little better. For example, one can see that a .170 ISO is about equivalent to a .277 BA which falls right at the median (50th percentile). It also illustrates that a .247 ISO indicates very good power, whereas a .096 ISO suggests a lack of power.

Figure 15: Percentiles for Rate Statistics in MLB, 2008

Percentile	BA	OBP	SLG	EOBP	ISO
Best	.364	.470	.653	.189	.296
90%	.306	.383	.530	.146	.247
75%	.293	.368	.500	.125	.217
50%	.277	.346	.449	.094	.170
25%	.258	.326	.400	.074	.127
10%	.240	.305	.359	.062	.096
Worst	.205	.260	.296	.032	.042

Data from Baseball-Databank.org

REPEATABLE SKILLS

If a player has a high degree of control over a skill and displays it consistently from year to year, it is said to be a repeatable skill. For example, a typical player will have a similar BB% from year to year. So the ability to draw walks is considered a repeatable skill. A non-repeatable skill is one which is more dependent on events outside the control of a batter. It is therefore difficult to maintain from season to season. Since BA tends to fluctuate quite a bit from year, hitting for average would not be regarded as a repeatable skill. A statistic which represents a repeatable skill is said to be a repeatable statistic.

One quick way to assess the repeatability of a statistic is to examine the correlation in performance on that measure between two consecutive years. A correlation falls between -1 and +1. If a measure has a correlation close to +1, then it is said to be repeatable. In other words, players who perform well by that measure in year one tend to do well on the same measure in the second year. Similarly, players who perform poorly by the metric in the first year tend to do poorly by that metric in year two.

If a measure has a correlation close to 0, then it is not repeatable, that is, a player's performance in year one tells us little about his performance in year two. A correlation close to -1 would indicate an inverse relationship between years one and two. For example, a low value for a statistic in year one would tend to be followed by a high value of the same statistic in year two.

I conducted a study including 428 players with 400 or more plate appearances in consecutive years: 145 players in 2000-2001, 134 players in 2002-2003 and 149 players in 2004-2005. Based on these data, correlations were computed for several batting statistics: BA, OBP, SLG, ISO, BB%, home runs per plate appearance (HR%) and strikeouts per plate appearance (K%). The results of the study are shown in Figure 16. Some readers might be surprised that K% (0.83), BB% (0.80), ISO (0.76) and HR% (0.75) were more repeatable than BA (0.43). This means that strikeouts, walks and power stats are more predictive of future performance than BA.

Figure 16: Repeatability of Batting Statistics

Statistic	Correlation
K%	0.83
BB%	0.80
ISO	0.76
HR%	0.75
OBP	0.67
SLG	0.67
BA	0.43

Data from Baseball-Databank.org

Using the 400 plate appearances cutoff created some bias because players who performed much worse in the second year might have failed to reach 400 PA in the second year simply because they did not do well. However, the 400-PA threshold was included to avoid small sample sizes. When the data were tested with lower PA limits, the correlations were a little smaller but not enough to change the conclusions.

PLATE DISCIPLINE

Plate discipline or strike zone judgment is an important skill in determining the long term success of a player. One simple definition of plate discipline would be the recognition of balls and strikes and the ability to react accordingly. In other words, swing at strikes and don't swing at balls.

Another way to define plate discipline would be the ability to balance patience with aggressiveness. Detroit Tigers manager Jim Leyland once said that he wants hitters to work the count and make pitchers throw more pitches, but he also wants them to swing when they see a pitch they can hit. Being able to maintain this delicate balance is an important skill.

Another aspect of plate discipline is a batter's approach with two strikes. Smart hitters will shorten up their swings a bit and concentrate on making contact once the count reaches two strikes. A good two-strike approach might also include fouling off strikes to extend at bats.

One simple way to measure overall plate discipline is to look at a batter's walk/strikeout ratio. If a hitter has good plate discipline, he should have a high number of walks compared to strikeouts. In 2008, the MLB average walk/strikeout ratio (BB/K) was 0.50 or about one walk for every two strikeouts. So, a ratio of more than 0.50 would be a good result for a player.

SWINGING INSIDE AND OUTSIDE THE STRIKE ZONE

Using Baseball Info Solutions (BIS) pitch data, which track the location and result of every pitch, FanGraphs.com owner David Appleman developed two new measures which more accurately represent plate discipline than BB/K ratio: OSWING% (percentage of pitches outside the strike zone at which a batter swung) and ZSWING% (percentage of pitches inside the zone at which a batter swung). These two statistics go along nicely with the earlier definition of plate discipline: swing at strikes and don't swing at balls.

CONTACT PERCENTAGE

Using the same BIS pitch data, Appleman also devised a new measure of contact hitting: Contact percentage (Contact %) is the percentage of swings on which a batter made contact. Interestingly, Contact% is much more repeatable than BA (0.92 year to year correlation for Contact% versus 0.43 for BA) and serves as a better measure of contact hitting ability.

ADDITIONAL PERCENTILES

The percentiles for plate discipline statistics are displayed in Figure 17. For example, we can easily see that a 0.89 contact rate is equivalent to a .306 BA, which every fan recognizes as good. Similarly, a 0.75 contact rate is equivalent to a .240 BA which is not good.

Figure 17: Percentiles for Plate Discipline Statistics, 2008

Percentile	BA	O-Swing	Z-Swing	Contact%	BB/K
Best	.364	0.15	0.82	0.94	1.93
90%	.306	0.19	0.74	0.89	0.90
75%	.293	0.21	0.70	0.86	0.74
50%	.277	0.24	0.65	0.82	0.57
25%	.258	0.29	0.62	0.78	0.42
10%	.240	0.34	0.59	0.75	0.33
Worst	.205	0.45	0.53	0.62	0.17

Data from FanGraphs.com

Illustration by Samara Pearlstein

Chapter 4

Total Batting Contribution

We know that Atlanta Braves third baseman Chipper Jones led the National League in batting average and on-base percentage in 2008 and that Adam Dunn drew the most walks while splitting time with the Cincinnati Reds and Arizona Diamondbacks. We know that Philadelphia Phillies slugger Ryan Howard belted the most home runs and that St. Louis Cardinals first baseman Albert Pujols had the highest slugging average. But which player was the best overall hitter? There are a good number of ways to answer that question and Chapters 4 and 5 will cover many of them.

ON-BASE PLUS SLUGGING

While statistics like isolated power and base on balls percentage do a good job of describing player skills, it is also sometimes useful to have a statistic that summarizes a player's total batting contribution. The most common summary statistic is on-base percentage plus slugging average (OPS) introduced by Pete Palmer in 1984. The OPS statistic is simply the sum of OBP plus SLG. Using data from the 2008 season, we can calculate Pujols's OPS:

$$OBP = .462$$

$$SLG = .653$$

$$OPS = OBP + SLG = .462 + .653 = 1.115$$

The idea behind OPS is that the two key elements of run scoring – getting on base (measured by OBP) and power (measured by SLG) – are combined to arrive at a number representing a player's total batting contribution.

Figure 18 shows that there was a strong relationship between runs and OPS for the 30 MLB teams in 2008. As a team's OPS increased, their runs went up in proportion. In fact, we can almost connect the points of the scatter plot with a straight line. This implies that the OPS statistic is a strong predictor of runs scored.

At the bottom of figure 18 is the same runs scored versus batting average scatter plot first shown in Figure 10 of Chapter 3. We can see that the points in the runs versus BA plot are not so tightly clustered around the prediction line as those in the runs versus OPS plot. This suggests that the OPS measure is a better predictor of runs scored than batting average. On an individual level, a player's OPS reveals more about his contribution to his team's runs than his BA.

Figure 18 – Runs vs. BA/OPS for MLB Teams, 2008

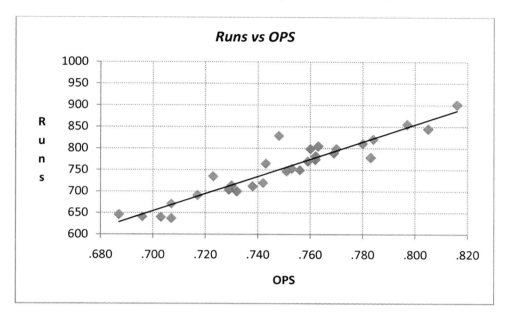

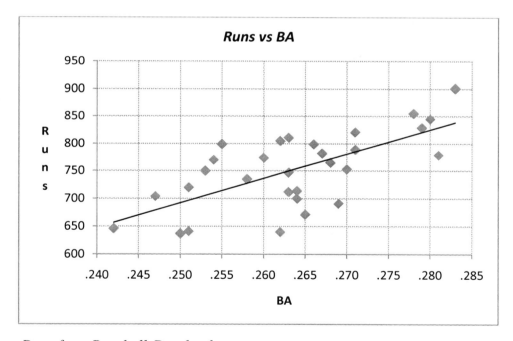

Data from Baseball-Databank.org

One of the advantages of OPS is its simplicity. Because of that, it has hit the mainstream in recent years. Figure 19 displays the MLB OPS leaders in 2008.

Figure 19 – OPS Leaders in MLB, 2008

Player	PA	OPS
Albert Pujols	641	1.115
Chipper Jones	534	1.044
Manny Ramirez	654	1.031
Milton Bradley	510	.999
Lance Berkman	665	.986

Source: Baseball-Reference.com

GROSS PRODUCTION AVERAGE

Pujols had the best OPS in MLB in 2008, but the OPS statistic is neither the only metric nor the optimal metric for determining the best hitter. Analysts have learned through the use of a statistical method called linear regression that OBP contributes about 80% more to run scoring than SLG. Since OBP and SLG carry equal weight in the OPS formula, this means that OPS undervalues OBP relative to SLG. Freelance baseball writer Aaron Gleeman (AaronGleeman.com) created a version of OPS with weights for OBP and SLG which more accurately reflect their relative contributions to runs. He calls it gross production average (GPA) and it is computed as shown below:

$$GPA = (1.8 \times OBP + SLG)/4$$

$$GPA \text{ for Pujols} = (1.8 \times .462 + .653)/4 = .371$$

In the GPA formula, OBP is weighted 80% more than SLG (1.8 versus 1.0). Some readers might also have noticed that .371 looks somewhat like a batting average and that was Gleeman's intention. Dividing by four puts GPA on the same scale as batting average, to allow us to more intuitively understand what's good and bad. Based on this, we know that a .371 GPA is outstanding and that a .220 GPA would be poor. The 2008 GPA leaders are listed in Figure 20.

Figure 20 – GPA Leaders in MLB, 2008

Player	PA	GPA
Albert Pujols	641	.371
Chipper Jones	534	.355
Manny Ramirez	654	.344
Milton Bradley	510	.337
Lance Berkman	665	.330

Data from Baseball-Databank.org

Despite the different weightings of OBP and SLG in OPS and GPA, both total batting contribution statistics yielded the same top five batters in the same order in 2008.

A limitation of both OPS and GPA is that they don't measure anything concrete. OBP represents the frequency with which a player reaches base and SLG is the average number of total bases per at bat. So, OPS is the simple sum of a percentage and an average and GPA is a weighted sum of a percentage and an average. Both measures work reasonably well in ranking hitters on total hitting production but they lack definition.

TOTAL AVERAGE

Total average (TA), developed by sportswriter Tom Boswell in 1981, is a relatively simple measure which is more concrete than OPS and GPA. In simple terms, it measures total bases gained per out. It is based on TB, BB, HBP, SB, H, caught stealing (CS) and times grounded into double plays (GIDP). It is calculated as follows:

$$TA = Bases/Outs = (TB + BB + HBP + SB)/(AB - H + CS + GIDP)$$

Pujols's TA is easily calculated from his 2008 numbers

PA	AB	H	TB	BB	IBB	HBP	SH	SF	SB	CS	GIDP
641	524	187	342	104	34	5	0	8	7	3	16

Bases = TB + BB + HBP + SB = 342 + 104 + 5 + 7=458

Outs = AB − H + CS + GIDP = 524 − 187 + 3 + 16=356

TA = Bases/Outs = 458/356=1.287

We can see that Pujols gained 1.287 bases for each out, giving him the best TA in the league in 2008. It should be noted that Barry Codell introduced a similar statistic (Base-out percentage) in the *Baseball Research Journal* in 1979. Base-out percentage is the same as TA except that it includes sacrifice flies and bunts in the calculation. The two formulas rarely produce significantly different results for the same player.

A limitation of TA is that it gives walks and hit batsmen the same weight as singles. In actuality, singles and walks are equally valuable in terms of putting runners on base. However, a walk can only advance a baserunner by, at most, one base. When first base is open there is no advancement on a walk. On the other hand, a single often moves a baserunner up more than one base.

RBI AND RUNS SCORED

OPS, GPA and TA are all useful for comparing the relative overall production of players but they don't tell us how many runs the player contributed to his team. If measuring runs is our goal, then why not just use runs batted in (RBI) and runs scored (R)? RBI and R are important contributions by players to their teams' offenses but they measure things that are, to some extent, out of the control of an individual batter.

Unless he smacks a home run, a player needs teammates on base in order to drive in runs. If a player has hitters batting in front of him who frequently get on base, then he is more likely to drive in runs than if he has weaker hitters setting him up. Thus, a player on a good hitting team has a better chance to drive in runs than a player on a poor hitting team.

A batter's position in his line-up also influences his RBI total. A leadoff hitter usually has fewer opportunities to drive home runs than a clean-up hitter, since the generally weaker 7-8-9 hitters bat in front of him. The RBI leaders at the end of a season are as likely to be the players with the most opportunities as the players most proficient at hitting with men on base.

The runs scored statistic has similar limitations as RBI. Unless a batter hits a home run or steals home, he needs teammates to help him score runs. Even a relatively poor baserunner will score a lot of runs if he gets on base frequently and has good hitters behind him. Who bats behind him in the line-up is as important as baserunning skill in determining how many runs a player will score.

The question at hand is not which player played for the better team or had the most opportunities but instead which one was the better hitter. How many runs would a hitter produce on a typical team? How productive is he likely to be in the future, independent of his team? RBI and runs do not answer those questions very well.

Another problem with RBI and runs is shown in the following hypothetical scenario involving the Detroit Tigers. Suppose Miguel Cabrera is hit by the pitch, Brandon Inge doubles him to third and Ramon Santiago scores Cabrera on a weak groundout. In this situation, Cabrera scores a run, and Santiago gets credited for an RBI but Inge, who delivers the key hit, gets credit for neither a run nor an RBI.

RUNS PARTICIPATED IN

If one does want to use RBI and runs scored to represent a player's run contribution, runs produced or runs participated in (RPI) is one option. RPI is the number of runs to which a player made a direct contribution. It is calculated by adding RBI and Runs and subtracting home runs:

$$RPI = RBI + R - HR$$

RPI was first introduced as runs produced in the 1950s by Sports Illustrated writer Bob Creamer but was recently renamed RPI by Tom Tango. If Boston Red Sox second baseman Dustin Pedroia doubles and then scores on a single by Kevin Youkilis, neither player actually produces the run by himself. Both participate in creating the run but neither is 100% responsible for producing the run. Thus, the name "runs participated in" is more appropriate than runs produced.

Home runs are subtracted in the RPI formula so that a player does not get credit for two runs (an RBI and a run scored) when he only participated in one team run. Many analysts including Bill James have argued that subtracting home runs unfairly penalizes home run hitters. They claim that a home run produces a full run and thus the hitter should get credit for both the driving in component and the scoring component. On the other hand, Tom Tango has shown, using linear weights theory (a topic that will be discussed in Chapter 5), that RPI with home runs subtracted comes closer to measuring a player's contribution to his team's runs than RBI + R.

RUNS CREATED

While the RPI statistic is a nice quick and dirty measure of a batter's contribution to runs, it does not solve the team dependence problems discussed above. There are numerous ways to measure a player's contribution to runs scored independent of the quality of teammates batting around him. One of the most common run estimators is runs created (RC), a statistic invented by James in 1982. One of the most basic RC formulas is based only on OBP and total bases.

$$Basic\ RC = OBP \times TB$$

Another way to state the formula is

$$Basic\ RC = OBP \times SLG \times AB$$

Note that James's first Basic RC formula actually excluded HBP from OBP but HBP is included in OBP here for the sake of simplicity. The computation of Basic RC for the 2008 Tigers is shown below.

$$OBP = .340$$

$$TB = 2,504$$

$$RC = OBP \times TB = .340 \times 2,504 = 851$$

The Tigers 851 RC total tells us that a typical team with a .340 OBP and 2,504 total bases should score 851 runs during a season. The Tigers scored 821 runs which were 30 runs (or 3.5%) less than their RC. It is useful to look at team RC because it is often a better reflection of a team's offensive ability and a better predictor of future performance than runs scored.

Figure 21 shows the accuracy of RC in predicting runs scored for American League teams in 2008. From the % difference column (% diff), we can see that RC fell fairly close to runs scored for most teams with only the Twins (+5.8%) and Red Sox (-5.7%) deviating by more than 5%. This tells us that we can estimate with fairly good accuracy how many runs a team scored just by knowing the frequency of easily measurable events: PA, 1B, 2B, 3B, HR, BB, HBP and SH.

A study of 414 MLB teams from 1995-2008 revealed that 43 teams had RC falling more than five percent from their actual runs scored totals. That is roughly three teams in baseball per year. Exceptions often involved teams that were either very proficient or deficient in hitting with runners in scoring position. A team hitting very well with runners in scoring position will often outperform its RC estimate while a team hitting poorly with runners in scoring position will typically fall short of its RC estimate.

Additionally, good baserunning teams will tend to have more runs than RC and poor baserunning teams will tend to have fewer runs than RC. Both hitting with runners in scoring position and baserunning helped the Twins overshoot their RC in 2008. The Twins were first in MLB with a .305 BA with runners in scoring position. Based on measures that will be introduced in Chapter 7, they were also a strong baserunning team

Figure 21: Runs Vs. RC for American League Teams, 2008

Team	Runs	RC	% diff
Minnesota	829	783	5.8
Los Angeles	765	754	1.4
Oakland	646	638	1.2
Cleveland	805	796	1.1
Baltimore	782	795	-1.6
Chicago	811	826	-1.8
Toronto	714	728	-1.9
Tampa Bay	774	796	-2.7
New York	789	813	-3.0
Kansas City	691	713	-3.1
Detroit	821	852	-3.6
Texas	901	936	-3.7
Seattle	671	698	-3.9
Boston	845	896	-5.7

Data from Baseball-Databank.org

On an individual level, the RC measure is a useful alternative to RBI and runs for determining a player's contribution to his team's runs. The advantage of RC over RBI and runs is that it measures a player's contribution independent of his teammates. The general idea behind RC is that scoring runs is a function of getting runners on base and moving runners along in a given context. There are many RC formulas and all take the form:

$$RC = (A \times B)/C$$

$$A = \text{Times reached base}$$

$$B = \text{Base advancement}$$

$$C = \text{Opportunities}$$

In the Basic RC formula (as we are defining it):

$$A = H + BB + HBP$$

$$B = TB$$

$$C = PA - SH$$

Pujols's RC can be calculated from his 2008 data:

$$A = H + BB + HBP = 187 + 104 + 5 = 296$$

$$B = TB = 342$$

$$C = PA - SH = 641 - 0 = 641$$

$$RC = (A \times B)/C = (296 \times 342)/641 = 157.9$$

This RC calculation tells us that Pujols contributed an estimated 158 runs to the Cardinals offense in 2008. The 2008 MLB RC leaders are shown in Figure 22 below. The first thing some readers might notice is that Chipper Jones and Rangers outfielder Milton Bradley did not show up in the top five as they did in OPS and GPA. While OPS and GPA are rate statistics unaffected by PA, RC is a counting statistic which gives a player credit for playing time. Jones and Bradley missed time due to injuries and thus did not create as many runs over the course of the season as the more durable David Wright of the New York Mets and Hanley Ramirez of the Florida Marlins.

Figure 22 – Run Created Leaders in MLB, 2008

Player	PA	RC
Albert Pujols	641	158
Manny Ramirez	654	143
Lance Berkman	665	132
David Wright	736	130
Hanley Ramirez	693	127

Data from Baseball-Databank.org

If one understands the Basic RC formula, then the many other RC formulas follow the same pattern. A more complex version (one of many technical RC formulas) includes additional offensive events – SB, CS, GIDP, SF, SH and IBB:

$$A = H + BB + HBP - CS - GIDP$$

$$B = TB + .26 \times (BB - IBB + HBP) + .52 \times (SH + SF + SB)$$

$$C = PA$$

$$\text{Technical RC} = (A \times B)/C$$

James revealed in the 1984 *Baseball Abstract* that the .26 and the .52 coefficients in the above formula were determined empirically to improve the relationship between RC and runs by teams. According to Technical RC, Pujols created 159.6 runs in 2008. This is not substantially different from his 157.9 Basic RC. Technical RC generally differs appreciably from Basic RC only for a player with a large number of stolen bases and a high stolen base success rate. In that case, Technical RC will give a significantly higher number than Basic RC.

RUNS CREATED PER GAME

If one wishes to compare the RC for players with different opportunities (a full-time player versus a platoon player for example), RC per game or per 27 outs (RC27) is useful:

$$Outs = AB - H + CS + GIDP + SH + SF$$

$$RC27 = (RC/Outs) \times 27$$

A batter's RC27 can be interpreted as follows: If every player on the team is cloned to the given player, that's how many runs the team would score per game. Pujols's RC27 in 2008 is easily computed from his raw numbers presented earlier:

$$Outs = 524 - 187 + 3 + 16 + 0 + 8 = 364$$

$$RC27 = (157.9/364) \times 27 = 11.7$$

So, a theoretical line-up with Albert Pujols batting in all nine positions, would have scored 11.7 runs per game.

OFFENSIVE WINNING PERCENTAGE

Another RC derivative is offensive winning percentage (OWP). A player's OWP is the hypothetical winning percentage of a team that has nine of that player on offense and an average pitching staff and fielding team, versus an entire league of teams with average hitting, pitching and fielding. It is based on RC27, league runs scored per game (Lg R/G) and the Pythagorean Theorem introduced in Chapter 2:

$$OWP = (RC27)^2 / ((RC27)^2 + (Lg\ R/G)^2)$$

Based on Pujols's 11.7 RC27 and the National League average of 4.5 runs per team per game, Pujols had an .871 OWP in 2008. Thus, a team with nine clones of Pujols in the line-up plus average pitching and fielding would theoretically finish with an actual winning percentage of .871 or 141 wins.

LIMITATION OF RUNS CREATED

A flaw of the RC formulas is that if one sums RC for all the individuals on a team, the result is generally not the same as team RC. In fact, the sum of the RC of the players on a very good hitting team will typically overestimate the actual team RC by a large margin. For example, if we sum the RC for individual Cardinals players in 2008, the result is 889 RC. If we instead, calculate their RC based on team TB and OBP, then the result is only 855 RC.

The multiplicative part of the RC formulas (A x B) assumes an interaction between getting on base and base advancement: OBP times TB. It behaves as if Pujols is batting in front of and behind other hitters who get on base and slug as much as he does. In reality, Pujols is surrounded by players who do not hit as well as he does. The result is that the RC statistic artificially inflates the contribution of great hitters. Thus, if one sums the RC totals of individual players on a team and at least one of the players is a very good hitter, the result may be more than the team RC.

BASE RUNS

The base runs statistic was invented by David Smyth in the early 1990s. This measure is based on the idea that we can estimate team runs scored if we know the number of baserunners and home runs and the typical score rate. The score rate is the percentage of baserunners that score on average. The basic formula for base runs is

$$\text{Base runs} = \text{baserunners} \times \text{score rate} + \text{home runs}$$

More specifically,

$$\text{Base runs} = A \times (B/(B+C)) + D$$

$$A = \text{baserunners} = H + BB - HR$$

$$B = \text{advancement} = (1.4 \times TB - 0.6 \times H - 3.0 \times HR + 0.1 \times BB)$$

$$C = \text{outs} = AB - H$$

$$D = HR$$

$$B/(B+C) = \text{score rate}$$

The coefficients 1.4, 0.6, 3.0 and 0.1 were chosen to improve the fit of base runs to total runs scored for teams. The base runs measure works very well for teams, even better than RC, but has a similar problem estimating runs contributed by individuals. Since home runs are separated out of the interaction between baserunners and advancement, the inflation for star players is less for base runs than for RC, but it still exists. One advantage of using base runs is that its accuracy for teams holds up well even for extremely high or low scoring teams and leagues.

THEORETICAL TEAM RUNS CREATED

James later got around the inflation of RC for star players by using a theoretical team concept inspired by analysts David Tate and Keith Woolner. James's idea was to put a player on a theoretical team of otherwise average hitters and then calculate how many runs the team would score with and without the player. The difference is the estimated runs created by that player. Using Basic RC as an example, the system works as follows:

1. Calculate RC for a group of eight average players. Using 2008 National League data, that is a team where every player contributes a .331 OBP and .413 SLG in a full year of PA (roughly 700 PA). Those eight players would create an estimated 673 runs.

2. Give 700 PA to Pujols and assume he bats at the same rates he did in 2008 (.462 OBP and .653 SLG) and add him to the team of 8 average players. That team would have an OBP of .345, a SLG of .440 and 840 RC over a full season.

3. Subtract the result in step (1) from the result in step (2) to get RC for the second team over the first team. The difference is 840 – 673 = 167. That is the estimated number of runs Pujols would contribute to this team with a full season of PA.

4. A full time player accumulates roughly 11.1% of his team's plate appearances. Pujols had only 10% of the Cardinals plate appearances so we need to adjust the RC obtained in step (3) above: 167 x (10/11.1) = 150 RC. So, Pujols would have created 150 runs playing on an otherwise average offensive team in the same proportion of team plate appearances. This is a more accurate estimate of Pujols's contribution to the Cardinals than the 158 figure computed previously by the Basic RC formula.

VALUE OVER REPLACEMENT PLAYER

Woolner developed the value over replacement player (VORP) measure, which is built off Basic RC and the theoretical team concept. In this section, we will discuss how it works in principle and how it should be interpreted. A more detailed discussion of the statistic can be found at Woolner's StatHead.com site.

First, we need to define the concept of replacement level players. When building a ball club, comparing players to league averages can be problematic. If a team is forced to replace a player due to an injury, he is not likely to be replaced by an average player or even a slightly below average player. In most cases, he will be replaced by a player who is substantially below average.

The replacement level is the expected level of performance the average team would get if it had to replace a player at minimal cost. Theoretically, this is the best player available who is not playing in MLB currently. A replacement-level player is a hypothetical player who hits as far below league positional average as the league backups do and is an average baserunner. There is much debate in the sabermetric community as to the proper replacement value of each position. Woolner says that the typical replacement level player used for VORP is roughly 80% as productive as the league average hitter at each position.

VORP is the difference between the number of runs contributed by a given player and a replacement-level player at the same position. An example of a replacement-level first baseman in 2008 was Chad Tracy of the Arizona Diamondbacks (.308 OBP and .414 SLG). VORP answers the question: How many more runs would a team of eight average hitters plus Pujols score over a team of eight average hitters plus a replacement-level player? Pujols had a VORP of 98.8 in 2008 which means that he contributed an estimated 99 more runs than a replacement level player would have contributed in the same proportion of his team's plate appearances. Baseball Prospectus also adjusts for the relative difficulty of ballparks, a topic that will be discussed in Chapter 14.

One advantage of VORP over certain other advanced statistics such as RC is that it considers that some positions are more difficult to fill than others. There are fewer players capable of playing MLB caliber shortstop than MLB caliber first base, for example. Because of the greater defensive responsibility of shortstops, they typically do not hit as well as first basemen. For that reason, VORP assigns a shortstop a lower replacement level value than a first baseman. This makes it easier to compare the values of players across different positions.

For example, if we do not adjust for position, Houston Astros first baseman Lance Berkman (132 RC) looks as if he contributed more to his team than Hanley Ramirez (127 RC) in 2008. However, if we compare Berkman to a replacement level first baseman and Ramirez to a replacement level shortstop, Ramirez has a 78.0 VORP and Berkman 73.5. So, by the VORP statistic, one might argue that Ramirez had a better offensive season than Ramirez considering the positions they played. One thing VORP does not do is consider how well players played their positions defensively. So, it can't be used to assess a player's total game. Statistics which take fielding as well as batting into consideration will be covered in Chapter 15. Figure 23 below shows that Pujols was the clear MLB VORP leader in 2008.

Figure 23 – VORP Leaders in MLB, 2008

Player	VORP
Albert Pujols	98.8
Manny Ramirez	83.2
Hanley Ramirez	78.0
Chipper Jones	76.2
Lance Berkman	73.5

Source: BaseballProspectus.com

A potential disadvantage of VORP is that the concept of a replacement player might be considered arbitrary, since it does not factor in the specific players available within a franchise's minor league system. A replacement level player on one team is not necessarily the same as a replacement level player on another team. As Keith Glab at BaseballEvolution.com pointed out, Philadelphia Phillies first baseman Jim Thome was injured in 2005 and was replaced by Ryan Howard who had a .567 SLG over 88 games. That is far above the production one would expect from the hypothetical replacement player. In general, though, a team that loses a solid regular player will have a difficult time finding a quality alternative.

EQUIVALENT AVERAGE

Another statistic summarizing the total offensive value of a player is equivalent average (EqA), which was invented by Clay Davenport of Baseball Prospectus. The raw version of EqA is calculated as follows:

$$\text{Raw EqA} = \frac{(H + TB + 1.5 \times (BB + HBP + SB) + SH + SF - IBB/2)}{(AB + BB + HBP + SH + SF + CS + SB)}$$

Some algebra would show that Raw EqA is similar to OPS with SB and CS added. One difference is the 1.5 coefficient for BB and HBP in the Raw EqA formula. Whereas OPS counts a single roughly twice as much as a BB (depending on the AB/PA ratio), Raw EqA gives a single a weight of two (one for the hits and one for the total bases) and BB a weight of 1.5. Thus, a single is worth 1.33 more than a walk in the RAW EqA formula. We will see in Chapter 5 that the Raw EqA weighting of BB's and singles is a better estimate of a player's contribution to his team's runs.

Some additional mathematics, including adjustments for ballparks, helps to translate EqA into a measure on the same scale as BA, to help users interpret the metric. As designed by Davenport, the average hitter will have an EqA of .260 (which is close to the all-time MLB BA of .262), regardless of hitting environment. For example, Pujols had an EqA of .371 in 2008. Even casual fans know that .371 would be an outstanding BA and it's an equally outstanding EqA. The EqA and VORP statistics can be found at BaseballProspectus.com for all players.

PERCENTILES

The percentiles for many of the statistics discussed in this chapter are shown in Figure 24. Those who are familiar with OPS can see that a VORP of 35 is equivalent to an OPS of .864 and that a VORP of 22 is equivalent to the league median OPS of .787.

Figure 24: Percentiles for Run Contribution Statistics in MLB, 2008

Percentile	OPS	TA	RC Basic	RC27	BsR	VORP
Best	1.114	1.286	158	11.7	149	99
90%	.897	.940	113	7.1	108	52
75%	.864	.868	95	6.4	92	35
50%	.787	.767	77	5.4	74	22
25%	.728	.670	60	4.5	58	10
10%	.672	.610	49	3.8	49	0
Worst	.584	.508	34	2.9	33	-17

Data from Baseball-Databank.org, BaseballProspectus.com

Chapter 5

Linear Weights

If you ever played youth baseball, you undoubtedly heard the popular refrain; "A walk is as good as a hit." In reality, a walk is not as good as a hit in all situations, such as when there are runners on base. Furthermore, not all hits are created equal. A double is better than a single and a home run trumps a double. Yet, in a simple metric such as batting average, all hits count the same. Just how much is each event worth in terms of scoring runs? We hinted at answers to this question in Chapter 4 but in this chapter we will get more concrete.

BATTING RUNS

In Chapter 4, we discussed several ways to estimate the total batting contribution of a player. In this section, we will look at another system of run estimation, called linear weights. The linear weights system is so central to modern sabermetrics that it merits its own chapter. The system was first introduced in *The Hidden Game of Baseball* by John Thorn and Pete Palmer in 1984.

In the linear weights system, weights are assigned to each batting event based on the statistical probability that the event contributes to a run. Tom Tango derived the following linear weights for the 2008 season:

1B	2B	3B	HR	BB	HBP
0.47	0.77	1.04	1.40	0.31	0.34

From examination of thousands of games, it has been determined that the average single contributes 0.47 runs. In other words, if one single is added to a team's hit total in each game for 100 games, that team would be expected to add 47 runs to their season total. The values for other events can be interpreted similarly. The weights are inserted into a formula to calculate batting runs (BR):

$$BR = 0.47 \times 1B + 0.77 \times 2B + 1.04 \times 3B + 1.40 \times HR + 0.31 \times BB + 0.34 \times HBP - 0.28 \times outs$$

In the above formula, outs are equal to at bats minus hits. The constant before outs (.28 in this example) is chosen so that the league average for BR is zero. It is generally between .25 and .30.

Note that there is not a standard set of linear weights. They vary slightly by analyst and by year. For example, Tango used a weight of 0.32 for walks for the 2007 season. However, the varying combinations of weights don't usually yield radically different results.

Batting runs is the number of runs a player would contribute to an average team beyond what an average player would have contributed in his place. We will use St. Louis Cardinals outfielder Ryan Ludwick's 2008 season as an example:

AB	H	1B	2B	3B	HR	BB	IBB	HBP	SB	CS
538	161	81	40	3	37	62	3	8	4	4

$$BR = 0.47 \times 1B + 0.77 \times 2B + 1.04 \times 3B + 1.40 \times HR + 0.31 \times BB + 0.34 \times HBP - 0.28 \times out$$

$$= 0.47 \times 81 + 0.77 \times 40 + 1.04 \times 3 + 1.40 \times 37 + 0.31 \times 62 + 0.34 \times 8 - 0.28 \times (538-161)$$

$$= 40.2$$

Based on the above calculation, Ludwick contributed 40.2 runs above what an average batter would have been expected to contribute given the same number of outs.

Some readers may have noticed that the weighting for hits in the linear weights system is different from that in the slugging average formula. By assigning the weights of one, two, three and four for singles, doubles, triples and homers respectively, slugging average inflates the value of different types of hits relative to one another. In terms of average run contribution, a double is not worth twice as much as a single and a home run is not four times better than a single. Instead, a double is worth about 1.6 more than a single, a triple 2.2 more than a single and a home run about 3.0 times more than a single on average. Additionally, a single is worth about 1.5 more than a walk.

LINEAR WEIGHTS BACKGROUND

Given the number of outs and the runners on base, we can estimate the number of runs that an average team would be expected to score in an inning. Palmer's original weights were based largely on simulation and only a limited number of real games but his estimates have been proven to be quite accurate by real game data. The situational run expectancy matrix in Figure 25 is based on the results of all MLB games from 2005-2008. It shows us the probability of scoring in each of 24 base/out states.

At the start of an inning (bases empty and no outs), an average team would be expected to score 0.534 runs. So, if it played 1,000 innings, it would be expected to score 534 runs. Suppose the leadoff batter on an average team in a given inning gets a single, putting a runner on first and nobody out. According to the run expectancy matrix, one can now expect this team to score 0.927 runs by the end of the inning. By getting the leadoff man on base, the team increases its projected run output by 0.393 (0.927-0.534). Thus, a single in that situation is worth 0.393 extra runs for the team.

Figure 25: Situational Run Expectancy Matrix for 2005-2008

Bases Occupied	0 outs	1 out	2 outs
Empty	0.534	0.288	0.109
First	0.927	0.556	0.240
Second	1.166	0.724	0.352
Third	1.478	0.976	0.382
First & Second	1.542	0.952	0.464
First & Third	1.822	1.192	0.514
Second & Third	2.046	1.447	0.618
Bases Loaded	2.383	1.634	0.808

Some information used in this figure was obtained free of charge from and is copyrighted by Retrosheet. Interested parties may contact Retrosheet at 20 Sunset Rd., Newark, DE 19711.

Not all singles are the same in all situations though. Suppose that there is a man on first base with one out. In that situation, the team would be expected to score 0.556 runs by the end of the inning. Then, the next batter singles to land runners on first and third. That scenario yields an expectation of 1.192 runs for the inning. So, in that instance, the single adds 0.636 (1.192-0.556) expected runs.

We can extend the process described above to singles in every possible base/out state. We can also determine how often each situation occurs over the course of a season. For example, there were 123,827 instances from 2005-2008 where there was one out and the bases empty and only 7,296 times where the bases were loaded and one out. Because it happened more frequently, the former situation will carry more weight than the latter in determining the average value of a single. From that data, we take a weighted average of the above probabilities (0.397, 0.636, etc) and arrive at .47. This means we expect the average single to be worth .47 runs. The process can be repeated for doubles, triples, etc.

HISTORY OF LINEAR WEIGHTS

The development of linear weights illustrates the long history of sabermetrics. As documented by Alan Schwarz in *The Numbers Game*, Ferdinand Cole Lane built a weighting system for hits long before Palmer created his linear weights methodology. Lane argued that batting average was an inadequate way of measuring the contribution of individual players:

"Would a system that placed nickels, dimes, quarters, 50-cent pieces on the same basis be much of a system whereby to compute a man's financial resources? And yet it is precisely such a loose, inaccurate system which obtains in baseball..."

Lane tracked the results of 1,000 hits to arrive at appropriate weights, and his eventual equation was:

$$\text{Total run value} = (0.30 \times 1B) + (0.60 \times 2B) + (0.90 \times 3B) + (1.15 \times HR)$$

So, a single was worth about a third of a run on average, a double 60 percent of a run and so forth. In a *Baseball Magazine* article in 1916, Lane compared Brooklyn Dodgers first baseman Jake Daubert, who won National League batting titles in 1913 and 1914 to Philadelphia Phillies power hitter Gavy Cravath based on his formula. Lane calculated a total run value of 79 for Cravath versus 62 for Daubert and concluded that Cravath was the more valuable hitter in 1915, an opinion not shared by many contemporaries.

In Lane's later work, he arrived at the following formula:

$$\text{Total run value} = (0.457 \times 1B) + (0.786 \times 2B) + (1.150 \times 3B) + (1.550 \times HR)$$

The weights in this equation are fairly close to those used in today's linear weights formulas. Lane also assigned a value of 0.164 for bases on balls. We now know that this is too low but it was better than the era's standard practice of overlooking walks.

In the 1950s and early 1960s, George Lindsey recorded detailed play by play data on over 1,000 baseball games and produced the first run expectancy matrix similar to the one shown in Figure 25 above. From that matrix, he derived the following weights for hits: 0.41 for singles, 0.82 for doubles, 1.06 for triples and 1.42 for home runs. Again, these numbers are not substantially different from those used today. In 1963, Lindsey published his results in the statistical journal *Operations Research* in an article entitled "An Investigation of Strategies in Baseball."

Lindsey used his method to evaluate a trade between the Tigers and Indians. The 1959 American League batting champion Harvey Kuenn went from the Tigers to the Indians in exchange for Rocky Colavito who smacked 42 homeruns the same year. Based on Lindsey's formula, Colavito and Kuenn had run values of 114.5 and 112.6 respectively in 1959.

Earnshaw Cook developed a similar situational run expectancy matrix in the 1960s independent of Lindsey's work. Cook applied his results to baseball strategy and published his work in *Percentage Baseball* in 1966. Among other things, Cook theorized that sacrifice bunts were generally a bad strategy and that the best hitter on a team should bat first to maximize his opportunities. While Lindsey used actual game data to arrive at his conclusions, Cook depended largely on complex probability theory and his work was largely inaccessible to most readers. Thus, his impact on the game and its fans was limited.

The first person to reach a wide audience with a run probability method was Palmer in 1984. While Bill James was the first person to really penetrate the mainstream with his work, Palmer's work was also very important in the advancement of sabermetrics. Palmer ran a simulation of all MLB games played since 1901 along with the play by play of 100 World Series games. Based on the results, he tabulated the frequencies of the offensive events and advancement values. He then calculated the expected run values for each event. What made his work different from the previous efforts of Lindsey and Cook is that he considered the negative impact of outs along with the positive influence of hits and walks. When a player makes an out, it brings his team closer to the end of the inning and reduces the probability that they score. The formula he devised is similar to the BR formula detailed above.

LINEAR WEIGHTS DERIVATIVES

As is the case for runs created, there are several derivatives of the linear weights methodology. Three popular measures were invented by Tango in 2006:

1. Weighted-on-base average (wOBA)

2. Weighted runs above average (wRAA)

3. Weighted runs created (wRC)

WEIGHTED-ON-BASE AVERAGE

Weighted-on-base average is a rate statistic like OPS except, instead of adding OBP and SLG, linear weights are used to reflect the impact of offensive events more appropriately. The base linear weights are the same as those used above in the BR calculation with additional weights for stolen bases and caught stealing:

1B	2B	3B	HR	BB	HBP	SB	CS
0.47	0.77	1.04	1.40	0.31	0.34	0.42	0.20

Taking those weights and applying some mathematics to the BR formula yields the wOBA formula:

$$\text{wOBA} = (0.71 \times (BB - IBB) + 0.74 \times HBP + 0.89 \times 1B + 1.26 \times 2B + 1.58 \times 3B + 2.02 \times HR + 0.24 \times SB - 0.51 \times CS)/ (PA - IBB)$$

wOBA is scaled to behave like on-base percentage, so one can know that .380 or better is very good, .340 is about average and less than .300 is poor (Tango also admits that the name wOBA was inspired by the "Monster in the Mirror" song on Sesame Street). Note that intentional walks are not included in the calculation. This is because they are usually issued in very specific situations and Tango felt that they have as much to do with game situation as with player value.

WEIGHTED RUNS ABOVE AVERAGE

If we know a player's wOBA, we can easily convert that to wRAA – a run estimator similar to BR. wRAA is based on the player's wOBA and the MLB average wOBA (MLB wOBA):

$$\text{wRAA} = (\text{wOBA} - \text{MLB wOBA})/1.21 \times PA$$

The 1.21 is a factor applied to render wOBA to the same scale as OBP for 2008. It varies from year to year but it is usually about 1.20. Why do we need wRAA when we already have BR which does essentially the same thing? The reason is because some analysts like the idea of being able to easily go back and forth between a rate statistic like wOBA and a run estimator like wRAA.

WEIGHTED RUNS CREATED

The wRC calculation shown below is based on a player's wRAA and the MLB average for runs scored per plate appearance (MLB runs/PA):

$$wRC = wRAA + MLB\ runs/PA$$

The wRC statistic measures the same thing as RC introduced in Chapter 4 but it is based on linear weights and does not unduly inflate the values of star players.

APPLICATION OF LINEAR WEIGHTS DERIVATIVES

Ludwick had the following statistics in 2008:

$$wOBA = .405$$

$$wRAA = 39.3$$

$$wRC = 113.3$$

One thing some readers might notice is that, for Ludwick, wRAA (39.5) is slightly lower than his BR (40.2) even though they are measuring the same thing. The reason is because of the inclusion of SB and CS and the exclusion of intentional walks in wRAA. The wOBA, wRAA and wRC statistics are listed on FanGraphs.com for every player in every season since 1974.

Baseball-Reference.com includes BR (listed as BtRuns) for every player and every season in the history of the game. Their numbers are adjusted for the home ballpark of each player. Ballpark adjustments will be discussed in Chapter 14.

PERCENTILES

Figure 26 lists the percentiles for the statistics used in this chapter next to OPS for comparison. All MLB players with 400 or more PA in 2008 are included. Based on this chart one can see, for example, that 75% of regular players had a wRAA of less than or equal to 22 and 25% were above that. It is also seen that a .371 wOBA is good and a .319 wOBA is sub-par.

Figure 26: Percentiles for Run Contribution Statistics in MLB, 2008

Percentile	OPS	Basic RC	wRC	wRAA	wOBA
Best	1.114	158	146	69	.458
90%	.897	113	108	28	.387
75%	.864	95	93	22	.371
50%	.787	77	73	6	.343
25%	.728	60	56	-4	.319
10%	.672	49	46	-12	.298
Worst	.584	34	28	-24	.264

Sources: FanGraphs.com, Baseball-Databank.org

WHICH TOTAL BATTING CONTRIBUTION STATISTICS SHOULD WE USE?

We have covered a lot of ground in the last two chapters and some readers may be confused as to what statistics they should be using to evaluate hitters. First, the calculation of the total batting contribution statistics should not be the end all for batting evaluation. It's useful to have an overall batting value such as OPS or RC or BR but these numbers do not describe player skills the way batting average, isolated power and walk rate do. Both total batting contribution statistics and the more descriptive measures of Chapter 3 are important in answering questions about player performance.

Now, if someone does want to use a total batting contribution measure to summarize a player's performance, which one is best? It really depends on how much simplicity one needs versus how precise they want to be. While we have detailed a few limitations of OPS, it is still a reasonable statistic for comparing the batting performance of players. It's easy to calculate and, for many purposes, the increased accuracy gained from a more sophisticated statistic is not worth the effort. If somebody wants to estimate the number of runs a team should be scoring, then the Basic RC statistic is sufficient in most cases. This metric even works reasonably well for most players – just keep in mind that it inflates the value of star hitters.

Those who want more accuracy should use a measure which does not overestimate the values of stars. Some performance analysts believe that base runs using the theoretical team concept is the most accurate representation of a player's contribution to his team's runs. The drawback is that the measure is not readily accessible. Others prefer VORP because it adjusts for position and because they believe that replacement level is a more useful baseline than league average. I prefer the linear weights system because it has a clear theoretical foundation and is the basis of many other statistics which we will discuss later. Two of the most popular linear weights measures are BR and wOBA. Fans not needing so much precision should employ the measures they feel most comfortable using.

Illustration by Samara Pearlstein

Chapter 6

Situational Hitting

Fans often complain that a statistic such as on-base plus slugging does not take into account game situations. For example, a double with a runner on second is more productive than a double with the bases empty. Moreover, a walk-off home run is more valuable to a team than a home run hit when a team is up by 12 runs, but they both count the same in the calculation of OPS. In this chapter, we will look at measures which give players more credit for getting hits in higher impact or clutch situations.

DO CLUTCH HITTERS EXIST?

For many years there has been a debate between traditional fans and sabermetricians about clutch hitting. Many fans believe that clutch hitting is an important skill greatly impacting the outcomes of pennant races. They also believe that clutch hitters are easy to identify. Sabermetricians, on the other hand, are much more skeptical of the impact of clutch hitters and of our ability to identify them. Some even doubt the existence of a clutch hitting skill.

A clutch hitter would be one who consistently hits better in high impact situations – with runners in scoring position, late in close games, etc. – than he does in normal situations. The challenge of researching clutch hitting is that any reasonable definition of clutch hitting will account for only a small number of a player's total at bats during a given year – maybe 30 at bats in a full season. Since we can gain very little information on player skills based on 30 at bats, it is virtually impossible to determine whether a player is a clutch hitter based on one season of data.

Many studies have been done to determine if clutch hitting is a repeatable skill which players can maintain over the course of their careers. The first clutch hitter study was conducted by Dick Cramer and published in *The Baseball Research Journal* in 1977. Looking at data from the 1969 and 1970 seasons, Cramer saw no evidence that clutch hitting was a repeatable skill and concluded that the clutch hitting skill, if it exists, had a negligible effect on the outcomes of games. Other analysts such as Pete Palmer came to similar conclusions.

With the availability of play-by-play databases such as those at Retrosheet.org, it is now possible to do more precise studies covering many years of data. In one such study, Andrew Dolphin looked at data from 1960 to 1992 and found that clutch hitting is indeed a real skill, and that it is possible to identify clutch hitters and chokers over the course of their careers. However, he also cautions that the skill is limited. A .250 batter will not become a .400 hitter in the clutch, but he may become a .265 hitter. Other analysts such as Nate Silver, who published his results in *Baseball Between The Numbers,* have revealed similar findings

While clutch hitting may be a true talent, it is not possible to identify clutch hitters without many years of data. This makes it difficult to forecast clutch hitting performance in the future. However, we do know which players performed well in clutch situations in the past year regardless of whether they possessed an inherent clutch hitting skill. Their hits in high impact situations did help their teams win games and should be accounted for in describing their past performance.

BATTING AVERAGE WITH RUNNERS IN SCORING POSITION

One of the most popular situational statistics is batting average with runners in scoring position (BA/RISP). It is calculated by dividing a batter's hits with runners in scoring position (second base and/or third base) by his at bats with runners in scoring position. A runner on second or third is considered to be in scoring position because there is a good chance he could score on a single. For example, Pittsburgh Pirates catcher Ryan Doumit had 44 hits in 108 at bats with runners in scoring position for a National League leading .407 BA/RISP in 2008.

BA/RISP has been used by some fans as a measure of clutch hitting ability. While it does tell us something about past clutch performance, it fails to consider the game state: the score, the inning, the number of outs, and the specific baserunners (e.g. bases loaded versus second base only). It also does not distinguish by type of hit (single, double, triple or home run). It is further limited by the fact that it is generally based on a relatively small number of at bats. Just as it would not be wise to judge a player based on 108 at bats early in the season, it is not a good idea to judge a player on 108 at bats with runners in scoring position. As such, it is not a good tool for projecting future performance. In Doumit's case, his BA/RISP dropped from .407 in 2008 to .216 in 2009.

RUNS BATTED IN PERCENTAGE

Another statistic which fans often use to measure a batter's performance in high impact scenarios is RBI. We saw in Chapter 3 that the RBI measure is limited by its failure to address opportunities. With that in mind, BaseballMusings.com owner David Pinto developed a new measure which does consider opportunities. Using data from Retrosheet.org and Baseball Info Solutions, Pinto determines how many baserunners a batter had a chance to drive home during the course of a season and what percentage of the time he was successful in doing so.

For example, if Texas Rangers outfielder Josh Hamilton comes to the plate with the bases loaded, he has three opportunities to score runners. If he doubles home two runs, then he gets credit for two successes in three opportunities. If he hits a home run, then that counts for three successes in three opportunities, as he does not get credit in this algorithm for driving himself home. Runs batted in percentage (RBI%) is the sum of a player's successes divided by his opportunities over the course of a season:

$$RBI\% = ((RBI - HR)/\text{runners on}) \times 100$$

Hamilton had the following statistics in 2008:

Runners = 474

Home runs = 32

RBI = 130

RBI%= ((130 − 32)/474) x 100=20.7%

So, he drove home 20.7% of the runners who were on base when he came to the plate. The RBI% leaders in the American League in 2008 are shown in Figure 27.

Figure 27: RBI% Leaders in American League, 2008

Player	Baserunners	HR	RBI	RBI%
David DeJesus	284	12	73	21.5
Shin-Soo Choo	247	14	66	21.1
Josh Hamilton	474	32	130	20.7
Casey Blake	228	11	58	20.6
Melvin Mora	406	23	104	20.0

Source: BaseballMusings.com

Pinto includes all plate appearances in his RBI opportunities. Another option is to do the same calculation but remove plate appearances where a batter walks, is hit by the pitch or gets a sacrifice bunt. The reasoning is that it is difficult for a batter to knock in a run if he is being pitched around or thrown at or is asked to bunt. One could make the case that some batters draw too many walks in spots where they should be trying to drive in runs, but it's also true that some batters get pitched around more than others. The American League leaders for this alternative RBI% statistic in 2008 are included in Figure 28. Figure 29 is the same as Figure 28 except it only includes baserunners in scoring position as opportunities.

Figure 28: RBI% Leaders in American League (BB, HBP, SH Excluded), 2008

Player	Baserunners	HR	RBI	RBI%
Casey Blake	193	11	58	24.4
Shin-Soo Choo	208	14	64	24.0
David DeJesus	254	12	73	24.0
David Ortiz	282	23	89	23.4
Josh Hamilton	425	32	127	22.4

Some information used in this figure was obtained free of charge from and is copyrighted by Retrosheet. Interested parties may contact Retrosheet at 20 Sunset Rd., Newark, DE 19711.

Player	Baserunners	HR	RBI	RBI%
Casey Blake	131	2	60	44.3
Shin-Soo Choo	105	5	51	43.8
David DeJesus	104	3	46	41.3
Joe Mauer	176	0	71	40.3
Justin Morneau	226	8	98	39.8

Data from Retrosheet.org

The first thing some readers might notice is that the RBI% leaders are not necessarily the same batters who were among the RBI leaders. Figures 27-29 also give us a hint that the three measures (Pinto's metric and the two alternatives) produce similar rankings. If we were to extend the list further than five names, we would see fairly strong agreement in the rankings of players on the three metrics. However, keep in mind that players with very large numbers of walks tend to perform somewhat better on the alternative metrics than on Pinto's statistic.

The RBI% statistics are all reasonable gauges of past performance in high impact situations. However, they are limited by the same factors as BA with RISP: (1) They do not consider the specific game state; (2) They do not distinguish between types of hits; (3) They are based on a relatively small number of plate appearances and, thus, are not good measures of future production.

BATTING RUNS ABOVE AVERAGE BY 24 BASE/OUT STATES

Batting runs above average by the 24 base/out states (RE24) is a relatively new statistic which does more to adjust for situational context than BA/RISP or RBI%. RE24 is similar to weighted runs above average introduced in Chapter 5, except it adjusts for base/out states. For instance, in the calculation of wRAA, a double with the bases loaded and two outs counts the same (0.770 runs) as a double with the bases empty and no outs. On the other hand, RE24 counts the bases loaded double more than the bases empty double (2.544 versus 0.632) because it does more to increase the expected runs scored in the inning.

RE24 for one at bat is the difference between run expectancy at the beginning and end of a play. For example, suppose Cleveland Indians outfielder Grady Sizemore bats with a runner on first and one out. In that situation, we would expect 0.556 runs to score by the end of the inning (based on Figure 25 of Chapter 5). Assume that Sizemore then doubles, putting runners on second and third with one out. In that situation, we would expect 1.447 runs to score by the end of the inning. Therefore, Sizemore's double is worth 0.891 runs

Summing RE24 over all of a batter's plate appearances yields his season total RE24. For example, Sizemore had an RE24 of 45.0 in 2008. So, by that measure, he contributed 45.0 runs above what an average batter would have been expected to contribute given the same opportunities. This is higher than his wRAA of 34.4, which means that Sizemore was particularly good in situations with high run expectancy and contributed more to his team's runs than wRAA indicated. The ability to consistently post a higher RE24 than wRAA is not a very repeatable skill. RE24 is a good statistic for looking at past performance. However, wRAA is a better indicator of future performance.

WIN PROBABILITY ADDED

The win probability added (WPA) statistic is another situational measure similar to RE24. However, it is measured in wins instead of runs. It also considers the score and inning, as well as the base/out state. WPA gives hitters credit based on the potential impact their at bats have on the result of the game. For example, an at bat in the ninth inning of a tie game carries more weight than an at bat with the team up by 12 runs in the ninth inning.

The WPA concept was first introduced as player win average in *Player Win Averages: A Computer Guide to Winning Baseball Players,* written by Eldon and Harlan Mills in 1970. Based on computer simulations of thousands of games, the Mills brothers determined the probability of an average team winning a game given the inning, score, number of outs and runners on base. They applied their methods to the 1969 season using play-by-play data purchased from the Elias Sports Bureau. The player win average measure gave players credit based on how their pitching or batting impacted the probability of winning games.

With the availability of databases such as that provided by Retrosheet.org, it is now possible to look at play-by-play results of games going all the way back to 1954. Using the rich resources now available, the win probability concept has been further developed by analysts, such as Doug Drinen (who coined the name win probability added), Keith Woolner and Tom Tango. Analyst Christopher Shea has calculated the win expectancy for every situation and provides these probabilities at his Walk Off Balk web site (winexp.walkoffbalk.com/expectancy/search).

The WPA measure gives players credit based on the effect each play has on a team's probability of winning. These probabilities vary depending on the game state before and after each play. They are based on data gathered from thousands of games and covering every possible situation. This system is an expansion of the situational run expectation matrix discussed in Chapter 5.

More concretely, WPA works as follows. Suppose the Indians are down by one run with a runner on second and two out in the bottom of the ninth. The average team has a 0.125 (or 12.5%) expectancy of winning the game in this hypothetical scenario. Now, suppose Sizemore singles to tie the game resulting in a 0.587 probability of winning. In this case, Sizemore increases the probability of the Indians winning the game by 0.462 (0.587-0.125) or 46.2% with his single.

In another game, the Indians are up 4-0 in the bottom of the eighth and outfielder Shin-Soo Choo bats with the bases empty and one out. Theoretically, this means that the Indians have a probability of 0.988 of winning the game. Now suppose that Choo hits a solo homer to make the score 5-0. The win probability is now 0.998, meaning that the home run adds only 0.010 or 1% to the win probability. So Choo's home run adds substantially less to the probability of winning the game than Sizemore's single and would thus carry far less weight in the calculation of WPA.

A player can also decrease his team's probability of winning. For example, suppose the Indians are losing 2-1 in the bottom of the ninth with a runner on first and nobody out. In this instance, they have a 0.331 probability of winning the game. Infielder Asdrubal Cabrera then hits into a double play which changes the probability of winning to 0.030. In this case, Cabrera's double play decreases the probability of winning by 0.301 or 30.1%.

Illustration by Samara Pearlstein

WPA is most often used to describe a player's impact over the short term, rather than an entire season. For example, it can be used to track the highs and lows of a single game as it progresses. This allows us to determine which plays had the biggest impact on the outcome of the game. WPA can also tell us which players contributed the most to winning a game or a short series of games, such as a playoff series.

WPA is also sometimes used to determine which players were most valuable to their team's win totals over the course of a season. Summing the gains and subtracting the losses in WPA for all of a player's plate appearances yields his WPA for the season. Figure 30 shows that Minnesota Twins catcher Joe Mauer led the American League with 4.88 WPA in 2008.

Figure 30: WPA Batting Leaders in American League, 2008

Player	WPA
Joe Mauer	4.88
Carlos Pena	4.30
Justin Morneau	3.89
Carlos Quentin	3.81
Grady Sizemore	3.47

Source: FanGraphs.com

One criticism of WPA is that batters do not have control over the game state presented to them. In the above example, Sizemore's single counts 47 times more than Choo's home run based on a game state which he did not create. The result is that a player might have a higher WPA than other players simply because he has more opportunities in high impact situations over the course of a season. WPA is also not very predictive of future results.

PERCENTILES

Figure 31 lists the percentiles for WPA and RE24 for all MLB players with 400 or more PA in 2008. Based on this chart one can see, for example, that 75% of regular players had a WPA of less than or equal to 1.92 and 25% were above that.

Figure 31: Percentiles for Situational Batting in MLB, 2008

Percentile	WPA	RE24
Best	7.51	73
90%	3.52	34
75%	1.92	23
50%	0.59	9
25%	-0.71	-4
10%	-1.52	-12
Worst	-4.11	-41

Data from FanGraphs.com

Chapter 7

Baserunning

The St. Louis Cardinals of the 1980s were almost devoid of power but Vince Coleman, Willie McGee and company generated runs with excellent baserunning. The Redbirds usually led the league in stolen bases by a wide margin and their stolen base success rate was generally high; However, there is more to baserunning than just stealing bases. For example, a good baserunner will go from first to third on a single or advance from second to third on a fly ball more often than a poor baserunner. At that time, however, there was no way to measure baserunning advancement other than stolen bases and caught stealing.

With the recent development of play-by-play databases such as Retrosheet.org, it is now possible to measure baserunning beyond stolen bases. With the availability of more detailed data, analysts now have the capacity to construct measures that more accurately evaluate overall baserunning performance. The addition of these baserunning tools to the batting statistics introduced in Chapters 3-6 gives us a more complete picture of the offensive production of both teams and players.

BILL JAMES HANDBOOK BASERUNNING

The first organization to publish baserunning measures based on detailed play by play data was Baseball Info Solutions (BIS). These statistics were introduced by Bill James in the *Bill James Handbook 2008*. The *Bill James Handbook* algorithm gives a player credit for the following types of baserunner advancement:

1. First to third on a single
2. Second to home on a single
3. First to home on a double
4. Wild pitch (WP)
5. Passed ball (PB)
6. Balk (BK)
7. Sacrifice fly (SF)
8. Defensive indifference (DI)
9. Stolen base (SB)

The system first computes the net base advancement on hits for each runner and compares it to league average. For example, Cubs speedster Ryan Theriot was on first base when a single was hit 30 times in 2008 and advanced to third 13 times (a 43% success rate). In the same situation, the average runner advanced to third 27% of the time. This means he would be expected to advance to third about 8 times in 30 chances. Thus, Theriot was 13 − 8 = 5 bases better than one would expect the average runner to be in the same number of chances going from first to third on a single. BIS does the same calculation as above for each player's chances of scoring from second on a single and scoring from first on a double.

BIS also determines how many bases a runner took compared to the league average on the following events: wild pitch, passed ball, balk, sacrifice fly and defensive indifference. A runner also gets credit for a base for every stolen base and debited two bases for each caught stealing.

In addition, this system penalizes a player for the following:

1. Getting picked off base

2. Running into an out

3. Grounding into a double play

Combining all of the above credits and debits on the different baserunning events, BIS determines how many bases each runner was above or below average. For example, Theriot was seven bases above what would be expected from the average baserunner given the same opportunities in 2008.

BASES GAINED ABOVE AVERAGE

Building upon the *Bill James Handbook* baserunning algorithm, I developed a similar procedure of baserunning measurement called bases gained above average (BGAA). The BGAA system includes many of the same baserunning elements as the BIS algorithm but adds advancement on ground balls and fly balls other than sacrifice flies. There is also no double play penalty in the BGAA system because I am not convinced that hitting into a double play is a baserunning event as opposed to a batting event. The complete algorithm is described below.

EXTRA BASES TAKEN ON HITS

One type of base advancement included in the BGAA system is extra bases taken by a baserunner on hits by teammates. There are three types of baserunner advancement of interest here:

1. First to third on a single

2. Second to home on a single

3. First to home on a double

A baserunner is credited with a base gained every time he advances an extra base in any of those three scenarios.

A runner can also be thrown out attempting to advance an extra base on a hit. When this happens, not only does the player use up one of three allotted outs in an inning, but he also removes himself from scoring position. Since being erased from scoring position is generally more damaging to run expectancy than simply failing to advance to scoring position, being thrown out attempting to advance carries more weight in this system than advancement. Based on the run expectancy matrix introduced in Figure 25 of Chapter 5, a player needs to advance about three times for every out attempting to advance to make a positive contribution to his offense. Therefore, three bases are subtracted from a player's bases gained total every time he is thrown out trying to advance an extra base on a hit.

Figure 32 illustrates the advancement on hits by Detroit Tigers outfielder Curtis Granderson in 2008. Granderson had 69 opportunities to take an extra base on a hit and was successful 37 times for a 54% success rate. He was not thrown out attempting to take an extra base on a hit.

Figure 32: Taking Extra Bases on Hits – Curtis Granderson, 2008

Situation	Opp.	Adv.	Outs
First to third on single	34	10	0
First to home on double	9	6	0
Second to home on single	26	21	0
Total	69	37	0

Some information used in this figure was obtained free of charge from and is copyrighted by Retrosheet. Interested parties may contact Retrosheet at 20 Sunset Rd., Newark, DE 19711.

In order to provide context to Granderson's advancement on hits, we can determine how many bases an average runner would have been expected to gain given the same number of opportunities. The MLB success rate for advancing an extra base on a hit was 35% (after adjusting for outs on the bases) so an average runner would be expected to gain 0.35 average bases x 69 attempts = 24.1 bases given the same number of opportunities as Granderson. Therefore, Curtis had 37 – 24.1 = 12.9 bases gained above average on hits (BGAAH).

BASE ADVANCEMENT ON GROUND OUTS

There are several situations that present opportunities for runners to move up on ground outs to infielders (including the pitcher and catcher). Let's concentrate on the three most common cases:

1. Runner on first base only with less than two outs

2. Runner on second base only with less than two outs

3. Runner on third base only with less than two outs

If a runner advances to the next base in any of the three above scenarios, then he gets credit for a base gained. Similar to the hits analysis above, a player is penalized by a factor of three for making an out while attempting to advance on a ground out in scenario 2 or 3. Figure 33 shows that Granderson had 46 chances to move up a base on a ground out in 2008 and did so 21 times without being thrown out.

Figure 33: Advancing on Ground outs – Curtis Granderson, 2008

Situation	Opp.	Adv.	Outs
Runner on first, < 2 outs	28	14	0
Runner on second, < 2 outs	12	6	0
Runner on third, < 2 outs	6	1	0
Total	46	21	0

Data from Retrosheet.org

MLB players advanced a base on a ground out 38% of the time so the average player would have been expected to gain 46 x .38 = 17.5 bases on 46 ground outs. Thus, Granderson had 21-17.5 = 3.5 bases gained above average on ground outs (BGAAG).

BASE ADVANCEMENT ON AIR OUTS

There are three scenarios where runners have opportunities to advance on pop ups, fly balls or line drives caught by outfielders:

1. Runner on first base only with less than two outs

2. Runner on second base (but not third) with less than two outs

3. Runner on third base (other bases may be occupied) with less than two outs

If the lead runner advances to the next base in any of these cases, then he gets credit for a base gained. As was the case for hits and ground outs, a player is penalized three bases for making an out while attempting to advance on a ball hit in the air to an outfielder. Figure 34 shows that Curtis was successful in 15 of 44 or 34% of his chances to advance on air outs and was thrown out twice in 2008. Since being thrown out twice is equivalent to failing to advance six times, his number of advances adjusted for times thrown out was 15-6 = 9.

Figure 34: Advancing on Air outs – Curtis Granderson, 2008

Situation	Opp.	Adv.	Outs
Runner on first, < 2 outs	15	0	0
Runner on second, < 2 outs	15	3	0
Runner on third, < 2 outs	14	12	2
Total	44	15	2

Data from Retrosheet.org

The MLB success rate on advancement after outfield air outs was 19% so one should expect a typical baserunner to advance 44 x .19 = 8.4 times in 44 opportunities. Therefore, Granderson had 9 – 8.4 = 0.6 bases gained above average on air outs (BGAAA).

BASE ADVANCEMENT WHEN BALL IS NOT HIT

A baserunner can also advance on plays where the ball is not hit anywhere. The most obvious case of a base taken on a ball not hit is a stolen base. Runners can also move up on wild pitches, passed balls and balks, and there is some evidence that such advancement is caused, in part, by baserunners distracting pitchers and catchers. Thus, good baserunners should benefit more from these events than poor baserunners.

Runners can also make outs on pitches that are not hit at all. They can be caught stealing (CS), picked off (PO) or thrown out attempting to take a second base after advancing one base on a wild pitch or passed ball. A weight of three was assigned to outs made trying to advance on hits, ground outs or air outs. Being caught stealing or picked off is usually a little less damaging because it most often happens when a runner is attempting to get into scoring position as opposed to already being in scoring position. In other words, he was standing on first base, not second or third, at the beginning of the play.

Many analysts believe that the break-even point for stolen base success rate is close to 70% based on run expectancy differences before and after stolen bases and caught stealing. This means that a player needs to steal seven bases for every three times he is caught stealing to make a positive contribution to his team's offense. This system weights outs on PO, WP or PB the same as CS. Thus, a baserunner is charged $7/3 = 2.3$ bases for each out due to CS, PO, WP or PB. As shown in Figure 35, Granderson took 20 bases in 2008 (12 on SB, 5 on WP, 3 on PB). He was thrown out six times, so we subtract $2.3 \times 6 = 13.8$ bases from his bases taken. This yields $20 - 13.8 = 6.2$ bases taken.

The number of opportunities also needs to be taken into account. This system uses times on base excluding home runs as a proxy for true opportunities. Bases Taken Average (BTA) is calculated by dividing bases taken by times on base. Granderson had a $6.2/223 = .028$ BTA, which means that he took .028 bases per time on base.

Figure 35: Advancing When Ball is Not Hit – Curtis Granderson, 2008

Situation	#
TOB	223
SB	12
WP	5
PB	3
BK	0
Bases Taken	20
Outs	6
Net Bases Taken	6.2

Data from Retrosheet.org

The MLB BTA was 3.7%, so the average runner would be expected to take $223 \times 0.037 = 8.3$ bases given the same opportunities as Granderson. Based on that, Granderson had $6.2 - 8.3 =$

-2.1 Bases Gained Above Average (below average in this case) on plays other than hits, ground outs or air outs (BGAAO).

TOTAL BASES GAINED

All of the types of baserunning advancement described above can be combined into bases gained (BG) to measure overall baserunning. For instance, Granderson had a combined 37 + 21 + 9 +6.2 = 73.2 BG in 2008. We could stop there and use BG as our measure of baserunning performance. However, we can do better than that. As indicated above, the problem with BG is that, like runs and RBI for hitters, it does not adjust for context. To allow for context, we calculate the total BGAA

$$BGAA = BGAAH + BGAAG + BGAAA + BGAAO = 12.9 + 3.5 + 0.6 - 2.1 = 14.9$$

Based on the above calculation, Granderson gained roughly 15 more bases than would have been expected by an average baserunner with the same opportunities. The best baserunners according to BGAA in 2008 are shown in Figure 36

Figure 36: Bases Gained Above Average Leaders in MLB, 2008

Player	BG Total	BGAA Total
Willy Taveras	99	58.6
Ian Kinsler	98	49.4
Jimmy Rollins	79	40.8
Ichiro Suzuki	112	40.5
Matt Holliday	84	40.3
Jose Reyes	98	36.3
Shane Victorino	77	33.9
Ricky Weeks	72	28.9
Jacoby Ellsbury	70	26.6
Nate McLouth	70	24.3

Data from Retrosheet.org

EQUIVALENT BASERUNNING RUNS

The BGAA method presented above is a substantial improvement over stolen bases or stolen base success rate but it makes some assumptions which ideally should be avoided. In the BGAA system, every type of base advancement is treated the same. In reality, base advancement is more likely in some situations than others. Specifically, the probability of advancement on hits, ground outs and air outs changes according to the number of outs and the location of the batted ball. For example, a runner is more likely to take an extra base when there are two outs than when there are no outs. He is also more apt to go from first to third on a single to right than on a single to left. Other factors that affect base advancement on balls hit in the air are batted ball type (fly ball versus line drive) and ballpark.

Former Baseball Prospectus writer and current MLB team statistician Dan Fox developed a more advanced method that uses the same baserunning elements as the BGAA system but more accurately weights different events according to the given context. For example, a runner gets more credit in his system for advancing on a fly ball to left in Fenway than he would in a park with more space such as Coors Field. Also, since it is generally harder to move from first to third on a single to left than on a single to right, a runner also gets more credit for that.

Fox also converts a base gained into runs using a version of the run expectancy matrix presented in Chapter 5. Players are given credit according to how their base advancement affects the expected number of runs scored in an inning. For example, if Red Sox speedster Jacoby Ellsbury is at first with one out, the team would be expected to score 0.56 runs in the inning. If Dustin Pedroia then singles and Ellsbury stops at second, that puts runners at first and second with one out. This increases the run expectancy to 0.95. If Ellsbury goes to third on the single instead, then the Red Sox would have runners on first and third with one out, a scenario which yields 1.19 expected runs. Since the difference between advancing and not advancing is 1.19-0.95 = 0.24 runs, Ellsbury gets credit for 0.24 baserunning runs by going from first to third instead of stopping at second.

Based on his algorithm, Fox developed new measures which can be found at BaseballProspectus.com:

1. EqGAR – Equivalent runs contributed by advancement on ground outs

2. EqAAR – Equivalent runs contributed by advancement on air outs

3. EqSBR – Equivalent runs contributed by stolen bases, caught stealing and pickoffs

4. EqHAR – Equivalent runs contributed by advancement on hits

5. EqOAR – Equivalent runs contributed by other types of advancement (PB, WP, Balks)

6. EqBRR – Equivalent baserunning runs

Granderson had the following Equivalent Baserunning statistics in 2008:

1. EqGAR = -0.21 runs below average

2. EqAAR = 0.89 runs above average

3. EqSBR = 0.65 runs above average

4. EqHAR = 4.17 runs above average

5. EqOAR = 0.31 runs above average

6. EqBRR = 5.81 total runs above average

According to this method, Curtis contributed about six runs more than would have been expected by the average baserunner given the same opportunities in 2008. Sometimes, there is a difference between the rankings of players on the BGAA and EqBRR methods. For example, Granderson was 3.5 bases above average on ground out advancement according to the BGAA method and -0.3 runs below average according to the EqBRR algorithm. The reason for this discrepancy is that the number of opportunities to advance on a ground out is relatively small and differences can occur due to the run value of a few high impact plays. The MLB EqBRR leaders in 2008 are listed in Figure 37. The EqBRR leaders are not radically different from the BGAA leaders listed in Figure 36. The only new player in Figure 37 who was not listed in Figure 36 is Los Angeles Angels speedster Chone Figgins replacing Milwaukee Brewers second baseman Rickie Weeks.

Figure 37: Equivalent Baserunning Run Leaders in MLB, 2008

Player	EqBRR
Ichiro Suzuki	12.3
Willy Taveras	11.2
Ian Kinsler	9.0
Jimmy Rollins	8.6
Matt Holliday	8.1
Jose Reyes	7.6
Jacoby Ellsbury	7.5
Chone Figgins	7.3
Nate McLouth	7.2
Shane Victorino	7.0

Source: BaseballProspectus.com

APPLICATIONS OF EQUIVALENT BASERUNNING RUNS

It is important to note that the best runner in baseball according to EqBRR – Seattle Mariners outfielder Ichiro Suzuki – was only 12.3 runs above average. The worst baserunner was Dionner Navarro at just 8.2 runs below average. So, there were just 20.5 runs, or approximately two wins, difference between the best and worst runners. Conversely, there was about a 105 run differential (approximately 10 wins) between the best and worse hitters using the batting runs statistic. This demonstrates the relatively low impact that baserunning has on wins and losses when contrasted with hitting.

BaseballProspectus.com also reports EqBRR for teams. In 2008, the New York Mets led MLB with 17.9 EqBRR and the Baltimore Orioles were last with -16.5 EqBRR. This 34 run difference, while not insignificant, is far less than the number of runs created separating the best and worst hitting teams (298 by Basic RC).

In Chapter 4, we saw that the Twins scored 46 more runs than their estimated RC in 2008 and we guessed that the primary reason for this disagreement was their excellent batting average with runners in scoring position (RC does not take baserunners into account). Another reason for the discrepancy may have been the baserunning events that are not included in Basic RC. Excluding EqSBR, the Twins were 15.3 baserunning runs above league average. This is an example of how the addition of the baserunning measures we've described here can help provide a more complete picture of a team's offense.

FIELDING BIBLE BASERUNNING RUNS

BIS owner John Dewan introduced the baserunning runs statistic in the *The Fielding Bible – Volume II* in 2009. His system is similar to the EqBRR system in structure but it includes fewer elements:

1. Base advancement on hits

2. Base advancement on air outs

3. Base advancement on PB, WP, BK, DI

It was built as a companion to technical runs created which already includes stolen bases and caught stealing. The baserunning runs statistic will be included as part of a total player contribution measure in Chapter 15. Granderson led MLB with +9 baserunning runs in 2008. Other results can be found at BillJamesOnline.com.

Chapter 8

Basic Pitching

Historically, fans have viewed pitchers through the lenses of wins/losses and ERA. Many consider 20 wins for a pitcher as the benchmark of a great season and fifteen wins as a good season. An ERA less than 4.00 is typically seen as good and an ERA under 3.00 as outstanding. On the other hand, anything more than 5.00 is regarded as sub-par. These familiar statistics can be deceptive though and may not tell us as much about pitchers as traditionally believed. In the next three chapters, we will identify the limitations of these popular metrics and explore alternative ways to evaluate pitchers.

EARNED RUN AVERAGE

Earned run average (ERA) is the average number of runs charged to a pitcher per nine innings pitched. To calculate ERA, we need to know the number of innings a pitcher pitched (IP) and the number of earned runs (ER) he allowed. An earned run is any run that occurred as the result of pitching and is not due to a fielding error (including one made by the pitcher himself) or passed ball. To determine which runs were earned in a given inning, an official scorer must re-create the inning as if the errors never occurred. If no errors occurred in an inning, all runs are considered earned. A run would be considered unearned in the following cases:

1. Batter reaches first on an error and later scores.

2. Baserunner remains on base due to an error on a play that would have retired the runner and then the runner scores.

3. Batter reaches base on a fielder's choice that removes a baserunner who reached on an error and the new runner scores.

4. Batter or runner advances on an error or passed ball and scores on a play that would otherwise not have scored him.

5. Runner scores after the third out would have been made.

The ERA of Boston Red Sox right-hander Josh Beckett can be computed using data from his 2008 season:

$$IP = 174 \; 1/3$$

$$ER = 78$$

$$ERA = (ER \times 9)/IP = (78 \times 9)/174.33 = 4.03$$

One problem with the ERA statistic is that a pitcher can allow a bunch of baserunners and runs in an inning without having them count against his ERA, because of one error made earlier in the inning. In the hypothetical inning described below, Beckett is pitching against the Toronto Blue Jays and the following sequence occurs:

1. Aaron Hill singles

2. Alex Gonzalez walks

3. Adam Lind lines out

4. Vernon Wells strikes out

5. Lyle Overbay reaches first base on an error to load the bases

6. Travis Snider clears the bases with a double

7. Edwin Encarnacion hits a two run homer

8. Beckett is removed from the game

In order to count the number of unearned runs charged to Beckett, the official scorer needs to reconstruct the inning assuming errors are outs. As a result, the inning is scored as if Overbay makes the last out of the inning and Snider and Encarnacion never bat. Without the error, it is assumed that the inning ends with two men on base and no runs scored. Thus, all the runs scored in this inning are considered unearned. Beckett allows a single, a walk, a double and a homer – resulting in five runs scored – yet no runs are charged to his ERA. This is not a well pitched inning by Beckett, but it lowers his ERA. Because of examples like this, some analysts have proposed Run Average (RA) as an alternative to ERA. RA is calculated the same as ERA, but total runs are substituted for earned runs.

PITCHING RUNS

Another limitation of ERA is that, like batting average and slugging average for hitters, it is a rate statistic not influenced by the pitcher's workload. Figure 38 shows that Beckett and Kyle Davies of the Kansas City Royals had similar ERAs in 2008 (4.03 and 4.06 respectively) but very different numbers of innings pitched (174 1/3 versus 113). Based on their innings, Beckett contributed more to his team in terms of run prevention over the course of the season. However, the ERA statistic makes it appear as if the two pitchers made almost identical contributions to their teams.

Figure 38: Josh Beckett vs. Kyle Davies in 2008

Pitcher	IP	ER	ERA
Josh Beckett	174 1/3	78	4.03
Kyle Davies	113	51	4.06

Source: Baseball-Reference.com

In order to give pitchers credit for quantity of innings pitched as well as quality, Pete Palmer introduced the pitching runs statistic in 1984. Pitching runs tells us the number of runs saved or lost by a pitcher compared to league average. It is based on a pitcher's IP and ER and the league ERA (Lg ERA):

$$\text{Pitching Runs} = \text{IP} \times \text{Lg ERA}/9 - \text{ER}$$

Pitching runs can be used to compare the contributions of Beckett and Davies in 2008:

$$\text{Beckett: } 174.33 \times 4.35/9 - 78 = 6.3$$

$$\text{Davies: } 113 \times 4.35/9 - 51 = 3.6$$

According to this measure, Beckett saved his team 6.3 runs more than the average pitcher in 2008. Davies, on the other hand, saved his team 3.6 runs more than average. Figure 39 lists the MLB ERA leaders in 2008 and shows how these pitchers compared on pitching runs.

Figure 39: Pitching Runs for MLB ERA Leaders, 2008

Name	IP	ER	ERA	Pitching Runs
Johan Santana	234	66	2.53	45.7
Cliff Lee	223 1/3	63	2.54	44.9
Tim Lincecum	227	66	2.62	42.2
Roy Halladay	246	76	2.78	42.9
Jake Peavy	173 2/3	55	2.85	27.8

Data from Baseball-Databank.org

A pitcher can also have a negative value for pitching runs if his ERA is less than league average. For example, Detroit Tigers left-hander Nate Robertson had -37.5 pitching runs in 2008 meaning he cost his team 37.5 runs more than the average pitcher.

LIMITATIONS OF ERA

A further limitation of ERA is that a pitcher has no control over what happens once he leaves a game. If he departs with a man on first with two outs and the relief pitcher allows a run-scoring double, the starting pitcher is charged with the run. In other words, a pitcher's ERA is dependent not only on the quality of his innings but also on the quality of the innings of his relievers.

Another potential concern regarding ERA is the timing of hits, walks and extra base hits. For example, if a pitcher pitches nine innings and gives up nine hits with each hit coming in a different inning, he will almost surely allow fewer runs than if he surrenders all the hits in one inning. If a pitcher frequently allows a lot of baserunners and extra base hits, he might get away with a relatively low ERA one year but it will almost surely catch up to him eventually.

A related issue to the distribution of baserunners is sequencing of events. Let's say a pitcher allows the following sequence of events in an inning:

1. Ground out
2. Single
3. Single
4. Homer
5. Strikeout
6. Fly out

In this case, he would be charged with three runs allowed for the inning. Now, suppose that Pitcher B has a slightly different sequence of events in another inning:

1. Ground out
2. Homer
3. Single
4. Single
5. Strikeout
6. Fly out

In this case, the pitcher is charged with one run. Both pitchers surrendered a homer and two singles but Pitcher B allowed two fewer runs just because the sequence of hits was different.

Some readers may be thinking that pitchers do have control over the distribution of base runners and event sequencing. They might argue that a pitcher could allow a lot of baserunners but limit the damage to his ERA by inducing double play balls or by pumping up his fastball to get a strikeout when there are runners on base. In fact, research by HardballTimes.com general manager Dave Studenmund has shown that some pitchers are indeed a little better at stranding runners than others over the course of their careers.

While it may be true that pitchers vary in their ability to prevent baserunners from scoring, research by Ron Shandler – author of *The Baseball Forecaster* and publisher of *BaseballHQ.com* – suggests that this has more to do with overall pitcher quality than clutch pitching ability. In other words, most pitchers who consistently strand runners do so primarily because they get strikeouts and limit base runners in all situations, not because they have a lot of control over clustering of base runners or sequencing of events. Still, the identification of pitchers that may have limited influence over sequencing of events is an interesting topic of future research.

PERIPHERAL STATISTICS

ERA is an important statistic to consider because a pitcher's job is to prevent runs. Because of the issues of reliever support, baserunner distribution and sequencing described above, however, it is a good idea to also look at peripheral or performance statistics. Some of the more popular peripherals are strikeouts (K), bases on balls (BB), hits (H) and home runs (HR). These statistics are often expressed as rates as follows:

1. Strikeouts per nine innings (K/9) = (K x 9)/IP

2. Bases on balls per nine innings (BB/9) = (BB x 9)/IP

3. Strikeout/walk ratio (K/BB) = K/BB

4. Hits per nine innings (H/9) = (H x 9)/IP

5. Bases on balls (or walks) plus hits per innings (WHIP) = (BB + H)/IP

6. Home runs per nine innings (HR/9) = (HR x 9)/ IP

Most analysts believe that peripheral statistics are more indicative of pitching skill than ERA because they are not directly influenced by reliever support or by the timing of hits and walks. Because pitchers have more control over peripheral statistics than they do over ERA, peripheral measures are also more predictive of future performance. We will see in the repeatable skills section at the end of this chapter that K/9 and BB/9, in particular, tend to be quite repeatable. If a pitcher has a low BB/9 one year, he'll likely have a low BB/9 the next year. Similarly, if he has a high K/9 one year, he'll probably have a high K/9 the next season. On the other hand, there is more year to year variability in ERA for most pitchers

As shown in Figure 40, the typical pitcher with 15 or more starts had a 4.22 ERA, walked about three batters (3.1) and struck out just over six (6.2) per nine innings in 2008. He also gave up roughly nine hits (9.2) and one homer (1.02) per nine innings.

Figure 40: Peripheral statistic percentiles for MLB Starters, 2008

Percentile	ERA	BB/9	K/9	K/BB	H/9	WHIP	HR/9
Best	1.65	1.3	10.5	5.3	6.8	1.00	0.38
90%	3.21	1.9	8.6	3.4	7.8	1.16	0.61
75%	3.68	2.3	7.7	2.7	8.4	1.23	0.81
50%	4.22	3.1	6.2	2.1	9.2	1.36	1.02
25%	5.07	3.7	5.2	1.7	10.2	1.49	1.25
10%	5.85	4.3	4.4	1.3	10.9	1.63	1.43
Worst	6.75	6.2	3.5	0.8	12.8	1.86	1.94

Data from Baseball-Databank.org

Figure 41 shows where Beckett ranked on ERA and on peripheral statistics among 68 American League pitchers with 15 or more starts in 2008. Beckett finished 27th in ERA but ranked much better on some of the peripherals – 8th in BB/9, 4th in K/9, 3rd in K/BB ratio and 10th in WHIP. His relatively good peripherals indicate that he probably pitched better than his ERA suggested that year.

Figure 41: How Josh Beckett Ranked in 2008

	ERA	BB/9	K/9	K/BB	H/9	WHIP	HR/9
Statistic	4.03	1.8	8.9	5.1	8.9	1.19	0.93
Rank	27	8	4	3	28	10	23

Source: FanGraphs.com

COMPONENT ERA

A pitcher's peripheral statistics can be combined into component ERA (ERC) – a statistic developed by James in the 1980s. Component ERA is a little complex but one can think of it as the ERA that a pitcher "should have had" based on hits, walks, hit batsmen and home runs allowed. It is the companion of runs created for batters and is computed similarly using pitching statistics instead of hitting statistics. Some analysts consider ERC to be more representative of a pitcher's true talent than actual ERA. One benefit of ERC is that it tends to be a somewhat better than current ERA at predicting future ERA.

There are many versions of the ERC formula, one of which was included in the 2009 *Bill James Handbook*. It is based on pitcher runs created (PRC), the pitching equivalent of RC for batters. Since it is difficult to find actual total bases for pitchers, the total bases (PTB) component of PRC is usually estimated from home runs and hits allowed:

$$PTB = (1.255 \times (H-HR) + 4 \times HR)$$

The complete PRC calculation is based on H, BB, IBB, HBP, PTB and the number of batters the pitcher faced (BFP):

$$PRC = (A \times B)/C$$

$$A = \text{baserunners} = H + BB + HBP$$

$$B = \text{base advancement} = 0.89 \times PTB + 0.56 \times (BB + HBP - IBB)$$

$$C = \text{opportunities} = BFP$$

The 0.89 and the 0.56 coefficients were determined empirically to improve the relationship between ERC and runs allowed by teams. Once PRC is calculated, ERC can easily be computed as follows:

$$ERC = (PRC \times 9)/IP - 0.56$$

In the above formula, 0.56 is an estimate of the unearned runs that the average pitcher allows. In cases where PRC is very low, it has been found that subtracting 0.56 in the above formula yields unreasonably low predicted ERAs. Therefore, one should instead multiply by 0.75 in those cases:

$$\text{If } (PRC \times 9)/IP \text{ is less than 2.24, then } ERC = ((PRC \times 9)/IP) \times 0.75$$

Beckett's ERC can be calculated using the following data:

IP	H	BB	IBB	HBP	HR	BFP
174 1/3	173	34	1	9	18	725

$PTB = 1.255 \times (H - HR) + 4 \times HR = 1.255 \times (173 - 18) + 4 \times 18 = 266.5$

$A = H + BB + HBP = 173 + 34 + 9 = 216$

$B = 0.89 \times PTB + 0.56 \times (BB + HBP - IBB)$

$\quad = 0.89 \times 266.5 + 0.56 \times (34 + 9 - 1) = 260.7$

$C = BFP = 725$

$PRC = (A \times B)/C = (216 \times 260.7)/725 = 77.67$

$ERC = (PRC \times 9)/IP - 0.56 = (77.67 \times 9)/174.33 - 0.56 = 3.45$

As one might have expected from his strong peripherals, Beckett's ERC was 0.58 less than his actual ERA. This is another indication that Beckett may have pitched better than his ERA suggested in 2008.

PITCHER WINS AND LOSSES

With a record of 12 wins and 10 losses, Beckett's 2008 season was viewed as a disappointment by some fans. The problem with using win/loss records to evaluate individual pitchers is that they are influenced so much by how many runs the pitcher's teammates score and how well his relievers pitch. Thus, win/loss record is considered by many analysts to be a team statistic and not a reliable measure of individual pitcher performance.

Back in the Deadball Era of the early twentieth century, pitcher win/loss records were somewhat more useful than they are today because pitchers during that era more often threw complete games. In 1908, 35 pitchers completed 20 or more games. In contrast, no pitcher had more than 10 complete games and only three had as many as five in 2008. Thus, pitchers of the Deadball Era were more responsible for winning and losing games than today's starting pitchers. Today, seven quality innings is generally considered to be a good start. More and more pitchers are yielding to the bullpen after just five or six innings.

If a starting pitcher pitches five or more innings, his team is in the lead when he is replaced and it remains in the lead the rest of the way, then he gets credit for the win. If a pitcher leaves with his team behind and the team stays behind for the remainder of the game, then he is charged with the loss. The following examples illustrate why using wins and losses to assess pitcher performance is problematic. If a pitcher gives up six runs in five innings and leaves with an 8-6 lead and his team keeps the lead, then he gets a win even though he has a 10.80 ERA for the game. Conversely, a pitcher can pitch nine innings allowing just one run and be charged with a loss because his team gets shut out.

In another scenario, the starting pitcher leaves with a 4-0 lead after seven innings and then the bullpen surrenders the lead. So, the pitcher pitches well enough for a win in most games but he does not get a victory because the bullpen is unable to hold the lead. While these examples are rather extreme, it is true that run support (RS) and relief pitching do play major roles in pitcher win/loss records. Consider the two groups of pitchers in Figures 42 and 43:

Figure 42: Fortunate Pitchers in 2008 (Group A)

Player	IP	W	L	ERA	RS
Vicente Padilla	171	14	8	4.74	6.2
Jon Garland	197	14	8	4.90	5.4
Bronson Arroyo	200	15	11	4.77	5.2
Kyle Kendrick	156	11	9	5.49	5.9

Source: Baseball-Reference.com

Figure 43: Unfortunate Pitchers in 2008 (Group B)

Player	IP	W	L	ERA	RS
Felix Hernandez	201	9	11	3.45	3.6
Jeremy Guthrie	191	10	12	3.63	4.3
Jake Peavy	174	10	11	2.85	3.5
Matt Cain	218	8	14	3.76	3.1

Source: Baseball-Reference.com

The four pitchers in Group A all had 11 or more wins and won more games than they lost in 2008. On the other hand, the four pitchers in group B all won ten games or fewer and had more losses than wins. However, every pitcher in Group B posted a much lower ERA than every pitcher in Group A. Most fans would agree that Group B pitched more effectively than Group A, but the wins and losses do not tell us that.

The lack of congruency between the win/loss records and ERAs of the pitchers in the above figures is explained by run support. The pitchers in Group A all received at least 5.2 runs per game from their offenses. However, those in Group B all were given 4.3 or fewer runs per game. For these eight pitchers and hundreds of others in the game's history, their win/loss records were determined more by the offensive performance of teammates than by their own pitching. This is why win/loss record is better viewed as a team statistic than as a measure of pitcher performance.

QUALITY STARTS

Understanding the shortcomings of individual pitcher win/loss records, longtime *Detroit Free Press* baseball writer John Lowe, developed the quality starts (QS) statistic in 1985 while working for the *Philadelphia Enquirer*. A pitcher gets credited a QS if he pitches six or more innings and allows three or fewer earned runs in a game. The idea is that a pitcher who does that will give his team a good chance to win the game on most days. The benefit of QS over win/loss record is that it is independent of offensive support.

The QS metric receives criticism from some fans as being an arbitrary statistic with questionable rules. People ask how a start where the pitcher compiled a 4.50 ERA could be classified as a quality start. One answer is that the MLB ERA in 2008 was close to 4.50 (4.46 for all starters) and that is the worst case scenario where a pitcher can earn a QS. Most quality starts are better than that and given the way pitchers are used today, getting six innings and three or fewer runs from a pitcher is generally a positive result.

Like any relatively simple statistic, the QS measure does have limitations. A pitcher could pitch eight or nine innings and allow four unearned runs, which many would consider to be as good as or better than six innings and three unearned runs, but not get credit for a QS. In *Bridging the Statistical Gap,* written by Eric Seidman in 2008, a new definition of quality start was introduced. Seidman suggested extending the definition of QS so that a pitcher who pitches 7 2/3 innings and allows just four earned runs is awarded a quality start. It might also be sensible to give a pitcher a quality start if he pitches five innings and allows two or fewer earned runs. Someone can easily make up his or her own definition of quality starts and count them by looking at pitcher game logs on Baseball-Reference.com.

Figures 44 and 45 display the Quality Start Percentages (QS%) – percentage of a pitcher's starts that resulted in a QS – for the pitchers in Groups A and B introduced in Figures 42 and 43 above. As one might expect, the pitchers in Group B all had better QS percentages than the pitchers in Group A. For these pitchers, QS% was a better reflection of their true performance than wins and losses.

Figure 44: Quality Starts for Group A

Player	GS	QS	QS%
Vicente Padilla	29	12	41
Jon Garland	32	18	56
Bronson Arroyo	34	18	53
Kyle Kendrick	30	13	43

Source: ESPN.com

Figure 45: Quality Starts for Group B

Player	GS	QS	QS%
Felix Hernandez	31	19	61
Jeremy Guthrie	30	19	63
Jake Peavy	27	19	70
Matt Cain	34	21	62

Source: ESPN.com

PURE QUALITY STARTS

As we discussed earlier in the chapter, peripheral statistics such as walks, strikeouts, hits and home runs are considered by many analysts to be better measures of pitcher performance than earned runs. So, Shandler developed the measure pure quality starts (PQS) which is based on peripherals. In the PQS system, a pitcher gets one point for each of the five criteria listed below in any game he starts:

1. He pitches at least six innings.

2. His hits allowed are less than or equal to his innings.

3. His strikeout total is at least as high as his innings pitched minus two. For example, four or more strikeouts in six innings or five or more strikeouts in seven innings.

4. He has twice as many strikeouts as walks.

5. He allows no more than one home run.

If the pitcher meets at least four of these criteria, he gets credit for a domination start. If he meets none or one of the criteria, then he is charged with a disaster start. Shandler says that a pitcher who averaged three or more PQS points over the course of the season likely had a good year.

REPEATABLE SKILLS

As described in Chapter 3, a skill is said to be repeatable if a player has a high degree of control over the skill and maintains it consistently from year to year. As for hitting statistics, we measure the repeatability of pitching measures using year-to-year correlations. A correlation close to +1 indicates that a measure is repeatable. A correlation close to 0 indicates that the measure is not repeatable.

Using the same method of correlation between two years used for batters in Chapter 3, I did a similar analysis for pitchers. In this study, 320 pitchers with 15 or more starts in two consecutive years were selected: 108 pitchers in 2000-2001, 99 in 2002-2003 and 113 in 2004-2005. The results are shown in Figure 46.

Figure 46: Repeatability of Pitching Statistics

Statistic	Correlation
K/9	0.77
BB/9	0.67
H/9	0.44
HR/9	0.38
ERA	0.33
Winning Percentage	0.25

Data from Baseball-Databank.org, FanGraphs.com

Not surprisingly, pitching measures tended to be a little less consistent than hitting measures and relief pitcher statistics (not shown here) were even more unreliable. The most repeatable measures for pitchers were K/9 (0.77) and BB/9 (0.67). Two of the most traditional measures – ERA (0.33) and winning percentage (0.25) – were found to be the least repeatable.

We can conclude from these data that K/9 and BB/9 are better indicators of future performance than any of the other listed pitching statistics. While we may not have a good idea of a pitcher's hit rate from year to year, we can be fairly confident that his strikeout and walk rates will stay relatively stable. Whereas a big increase in H/9 might be due to bad fielding or misfortune, a substantial increase in BB/9 or decrease in K/9 is an indicator that the pitcher did not pitch as well as he did previously.

WRAP-UP

In this chapter, we covered some of the limitations of the ERA and individual pitcher win/loss record statistics and discussed some alternative measures. However, we have still done little to separate pitching from fielding. Every time a ball is put into play, the responsibility must be shared by the pitcher and fielder. In Chapter 9, we will explore how pitcher performance can be isolated from fielding support.

Chapter 9

Fielding Independent Pitching

Imagine a pitcher supported by infielders who seize every ground ball in sight and outfielders who chase down fly balls from foul line to foul line. With a strong defense like that behind him, the pitcher can allow the batters to put the ball in play and let his fielders do the work. Now imagine the same hurler surrounded by infielders who let balls go through the holes and slow footed outfielders who can't reach fly balls in the gaps or over their heads. Most fans would agree that this pitcher will give up more hits, extra base hits and runs in this scenario than in the first scenario. Fielders can have a substantial influence on the success of pitchers, but traditional pitching statistics do not take that into account.

The goal of every baseball team when it is in the field is to give up as few runs as possible and this, of course, is done with pitching and fielding. The challenge is to properly assign run prevention to pitchers versus fielders, so we can evaluate each phase of the game separately and fairly. This can be tricky since pitching and fielding are so intertwined, but much progress has been made in recent years.

THE DIPS THEORY

In Chapter 8, we discussed how ERA can be influenced by factors that are at least partly beyond the control of a pitcher, such as relief pitcher support, distribution of baserunners and sequencing of events. ERA is further limited by the fact that it does not take into account the ability of fielders to get to balls.

In an article entitled "Pitchers and Defense: How much control do hurlers have?" published at Baseball Prospectus in 2001, researcher Voros McCracken presented his Defense Independent Pitching Statistics (DIPS) theory. The results of his study suggested that there is surprisingly little difference among pitchers in their ability to prevent hits on balls put into the field of play and that hits allowed are not very meaningful in the evaluation of a pitcher. Specifically, he revealed that there is very little correlation between pitcher quality and the relative frequency of hits allowed on balls in play. He also showed that pitchers have much less control over hits allowed than they do over defense independent events like walks and strikeouts.

McCracken's somewhat counter-intuitive conclusions were met with much skepticism, even in the sabermetric community. Tom Tippett, the creator of the popular Diamond Mind simulation game, did an extensive study in 2003 which revealed that some pitchers such as Tom Glavine and Jamie Moyer have been consistently above average in terms of preventing hits on balls in play. Tippett also found that knuckleball pitchers, in general, had been particularly good at limiting hits. Two examples are Charlie Hough and Phil Niekro.

Mitchel Lichtman further challenged McCracken's conclusions in a study of the impact of batted ball types on hits on balls in play in 2004. Lichtman found that pitchers had a good deal of control over how many ground balls and fly balls (in both the infield and outfield) they allowed and that ground balls were more likely to be hits than fly balls. To confirm these results, I looked at data from all MLB games in 2005-2008. I found that batters hit for a .243 BA on ground balls and a .142 BA on fly balls in play. I excluded home runs because they are usually not playable at all and line drives because they are generally much less playable than ground balls and fly balls.

While McCracken may have originally underestimated the influence of pitchers on batted balls, his basic idea has been shown to be largely correct. For most pitchers, preventing hits on balls in play appears to be as much or more a function of random luck or fielders making plays as it is the ability of the pitchers to induce easy to field balls. While some pitchers do have a significant ability to induce more "field-able" batted balls than others, most pitchers have much less control over what happens on balls in play than they do over strikeouts and walks.

BATTING AVERAGE ON BALLS IN PLAY

Batting average on balls in play (BABIP) is simply the percentage of balls put in play excluding homers which result in hits. The ideal formula for BABIP would look something like:

$$BABIP = (H - HR)/ (\text{plays resulting in outs} + H - HR - K)$$

However, we can't simply multiply innings pitched by three to get plays resulting in outs because double plays need to be considered. Data for pitcher double plays are not easily accessible but it is known that the average pitcher induces approximately 0.18 double plays per inning. So, we can estimate that there are $3.00 - 0.18 = 2.82$ plays resulting in outs per inning on average. Based on that, the most commonly used BABIP formula is:

$$BABIP = (H - HR)/ (IP \times 2.82 + H - HR - K)$$

Joe Blanton compiled the following statistics pitching for the Oakland Athletics in 2005:

IP	HR	BB	IBB	HBP	K	H	ERA
201 1/3	23	64	3	5	116	178	3.53

If we plug Blanton's numbers into the formula, we see that his BABIP was .255:

$$BABIP = (H - HR)/ (IP \times 2.82 + H - HR - K)$$

$$= (178 - 23)/ (201.33 \times 2.82 + 178 - 23 - 116) = .255$$

Compared to other statistics such as bases on balls per inning (BB/IP) and strikeouts per inning (K/IP) over which pitchers have more control, BABIP does not vary a great deal among pitchers. As shown in Figure 47 below, the BABIP of starting pitchers in 2005 ranged from .252 to .343 with the median falling at .295. The middle 50% percent of pitchers ranged from .287 to .307, which is a relatively small interval for such a large group of pitchers.

Figure 47: Percentiles for BABIP and BB per Inning, 2005

Percentile	BABIP	BB/IP
Best	.252	.048
90%	.268	.192
75%	.287	.233
50%	.295	.289
25%	.307	.333
10%	.322	.381
Worst	.343	.544

Data from Baseball-Databank.org

In contrast to BABIP, pitchers varied much more on BB/IP. BB/IP had almost the same median (.289) as BABIP but it had a much different distribution. BBIP ranged from .048 to .544 and the middle 50 percent of pitchers fell between .233 and .333, a much wider interval than that for BABIP. In fact, the distribution of BB/IP was five more times disperse than that of BABIP. Similarly, K/IP had four times as much variation as BABIP.

Because the distribution of BABIP is so tight, a very low BABIP is considered to be a red flag. A pitcher (even a very good one) with a really low BABIP (e.g. .255) in a given season will have a difficult time maintaining such a low BABIP the following season. This is because he probably had some good luck in terms of fielders making plays in the first season and we would not expect him to continue to be so fortunate in the future. That combined with the fact that ERA and BABIP are positively correlated means that such a pitcher will more than likely see both his BABIP and ERA increase in the following season.

Figure 48 shows a comparison between Blanton's 2005 and 2006 seasons.   Blanton had similar HR/9, BB/9 and K/9 rates in 2005 and 2006 but his BABIP soared from .255 to .337. The change in BABIP also showed up in his H/9 rates: 8.0 in 2005 and 11.2 in 2006. Consequently, his ERA rose from 3.53 in 2005 to 4.82 in 2006.

Figure 48: A Comparison of Joe Blanton's 2005 and 2006 seasons

Year	IP	HR/9	BB/9	K/9	H/9	BABIP	ERA
2005	201 1/3	1.0	2.9	5.2	8.0	.255	3.53
2006	194 1/3	0.8	2.7	5.0	11.2	.337	4.82

Source: FanGraphs.com

Such a wide swing in BABIP suggests that Blanton had better luck in 2005 than 2006 and defense may have been part of his good fortune. Based on fielding statistics which will be discussed in Chapters 11-13, the Athletics had a better fielding team in 2005 than in 2006. This probably explains some of the difference

To show that Blanton's situation was not unique, I looked at 508 MLB pitchers between 1995 and 2008 who pitched for the same team and accumulated at least 162 innings in two consecutive seasons. Of the 40 pitchers with BABIPs of .265 or lower in year one, 31 had higher ERAs in year two. In fact, the ERA of those 31 pitchers rose by almost a run on average in the second year.

What about pitchers with unusually high BABIPs? Can we expect their ERAs to go down the next season? To a certain extent yes, but the trend is not as strong as that for low BABIP pitchers. Of the 40 pitchers with BABIPs of .326 or more in the first season, 25 improved their ERAs in the second season by an average of 0.86 runs. While an extremely low BABIP is most likely the result of good fortune, a really high BABIP may be an indication that the pitcher was simply hit hard.

FIELDING INDEPENDENT PITCHING ERA

With McCracken's DIPS theory in mind, Tom Tango created the fielding independent pitching ERA (FIP) measure from items the pitcher essentially controls: K, BB, HR and HBP. The formula for FIP is

$$FIP = (HR \times 13 + (BB + HBP - IBB) \times 3 - K \times 2)/IP + C$$

C is a league specific factor (usually around 3.20) which makes FIP read like an ERA. It is used so that the average FIP will equal the average ERA, which makes FIP easier for fans to understand and interpret. Even if one finds the calculation to be complex, just think of FIP as the ERA that a pitcher "should have had" based on events which are primarily his responsibility: K, BB, HBP and HR. FIP differs from Bill James's ERC of Chapter 8 in that it does not include hits in the calculation. Hits are excluded from FIP because they are not considered fielding independent events, that is, both pitchers and fielders share the responsibility for hits allowed.

Because FIP is based only on events essentially controlled by a pitcher, it eliminates some of the luck involved in ERA. For example, a pitcher may have a low ERA because of things largely beyond his influence such as fortuitous distribution of baserunners or sequencing of events discussed in Chapter 8. Additionally, he may have been backed by unusually great fielding plays or by hard-hit balls luckily hit directly at fielders. Conversely, a pitcher with a high ERA might have been the victim of unfortunate distribution of baserunners or sequencing of events, poor defense or a large number of softly hit balls that fell for hits. FIP, on the other hand, is only influenced by factors that are primarily the responsibility of the pitcher. The benefit of FIP is that it is a somewhat better predictor of future ERA than is current ERA. FIP is also believed by many analysts to be a better indicator of real talent.

Blanton's 3.53 ERA in 2005 was substantially better than the league average, but his 5.2 K/9 was below average and his 1.03 HR/9 and 2.9 BB/9 were only about average. Because his fielding independent statistics were middling, we would expect his FIP to be similarly mediocre. Blanton's FIP is calculated below:

C=3.07 for the American League in 2008

$$FIP = (HR \times 13 + (BB + HBP - IBB) \times 3 - K \times 2)/IP + C$$

$$= 23 \times 13 + (67 + 5 - 3) \times 3 - 116 \times 2)/201.33 + 3.07 = 4.43$$

Blanton's 4.43 FIP was nearly a run higher than his ERA of 3.53 which suggests that he was probably not as effective as his ERA indicated in 2005.

BATTED BALL DATA

One of the most important advances in modern statistics has been the tracking of batted ball data. Thanks to companies such as Sports Team Analysis and Tracking Systems (STATS, Inc.) and BIS, we now have access to measures such as groundball percentage (GB%) – the percentage of batted balls which result in ground balls. Other batted ball statistics include line drive percentage (LD%), outfield fly ball percentage (OFF%) and infield fly percentage (IFF%). These data are particularly useful for evaluation of pitchers because it is known that inducing batters to hit ground balls will typically yield more favorable results than allowing large numbers of line drives or outfield flies.

Figure 49 presents the BA and SLG by batted ball type for all MLB games in 2005-2008. It shows that batters hit for a .243 BA and .264 SLG on ground balls. In contrast, balls hit in the air (including line drives, outfield flies and infield flies) yielded a .400 BA and .733 slugging average. The most destructive types of batted balls were line drives (.732 BA and 1.005 SLG) and outfield fly balls (.280, .751). Infield flies were relative harmless (.022, .027) but they were less common than line drives and outfield flies. From these data, we can see that it is generally beneficial for a pitcher to induce a large number of ground balls relative to balls hit in the air.

Figure 49: BA and SLG by Batted Ball Type, 2005-2008

Event	BA	SLG
LD	.732	1.005
OFF	.280	.751
IFF	.022	.027
GB	.243	.264
Any Air	.400	.733

Some information used in this figure was obtained free of charge from and is copyrighted by Retrosheet. Interested parties may contact Retrosheet at 20 Sunset Rd., Newark, DE 19711.

The top five ground-ball rates among MLB pitchers in 2008 are listed in Figure 50. The GB% metric and other batted ball data can be found at FanGraphs.com.

Figure 50: GB% Leaders in MLB, 2008

Pitcher	GB%
Brandon Webb	64.2
Derek Lowe	60.3
Aaron Cook	55.9
Ubaldo Jimenez	54.4
John Lannan	54.2

QUICK ERA

One of the criticisms of the FIP statistic covered earlier in the chapter is that it only includes BB, K, HBP and HR and does not adequately address a pitcher's ability to induce ground balls. The quick ERA (QERA) statistic, developed by Baseball Prospectus writer and political polling analyst Nate Silver, is similar to FIP but it uses GB% instead of home runs. The advantage of GB% over home runs is that ground balls are less park dependent than home runs. Another favorable characteristic of GB% is that it is a fairly repeatable statistic – a year-to-year correlation of 0.73 using the method introduced in Chapter 3. This makes it a good measure for projection. Conversely, pitcher home run rate tends to fluctuate a lot from season to season because pitchers do not have a great deal of control over how far fly balls are hit. The formula for QERA is:

$$QERA = (2.69 - SO\% \times 3.40 + BB\% \times 3.88 - GB\% \times 0.66)^2$$

Silver derived the model for QERA by using regression analysis to determine the coefficients (2.69, 3.40, 3.88 and 0.66) which yield the best estimate of ERA.

Blanton had the following numbers in 2005:

BFP	BB%	K%	GB%	QERA
835	.077	.139	.447	4.93

As we saw with FIP, Blanton's QERA was a lot higher than his actual 2005 ERA (3.53).

A limitation of QERA is that ground balls are not as fielding independent as home runs. While a pitcher has a good deal of control over his ground ball rate, he has less influence on the ability of fielders to convert the grounders into outs.

Another potential issue in theory is that QERA does not work well for pitchers with extremely high or low batted ball rates. For example, if a pitcher allowed just four batted balls during a season and three of them were ground balls, that would be a 75% ground ball rate and it would unduly deflate his QERA as if he was an extreme ground ball pitcher. However, QERA presents no such problem for the vast majority of pitchers with a full season of innings.

EXPECTED FIP

Research by David Studenmund has shown that pitchers have more control over how many fly balls they allow than how many home runs they give up. He determined that pitchers do not typically maintain consistency on their annual numbers of home runs per fly ball (HR/FB) and that the rate is roughly 11% across MLB, depending on ballparks. As a result, a pitcher with a really high HR/FB rate in a particular year (e.g. John Lackey of the Angels had a 16.6% rate in 2008), would not be expected to match that rate in the future. The same can be said for a pitcher with a really low home run to fly ball rate (e.g. Ryan Dempster of the Cubs had a 7.6% rate in 2008).

Because fly ball rate is a better indicator of true talent than home runs, Studenmund developed the expected FIP (xFIP) statistic which includes fly balls rather than home runs. In the xFIP calculation, each pitcher is assumed to have the league average HR/FB (Lg HR/FB). That rate (usually around 0.11) is multiplied by the pitcher's number of fly balls allowed:

$$xFIP = ((FB \times Lg\ HR/FB) \times 13 + (BB + HBP - IBB) \times 3 - K \times 2)/IP + C$$

C is chosen so that xFIP is equivalent to ERA. The xFIP statistic can be found for all pitchers in all seasons since 2000 at FanGraphs.com. Colin Wyers, a writer for HardballTimes.com showed that xFIP is a marginally better predictor of future ERA than FIP. The drawback of xFIP is that it does not describe a pitcher's actual past performance as well as FIP. If a pitcher allowed an unusually large number of home runs per fly ball, that reflects poorly on his past record even though it might not be predictive of future results.

tRA

One of the criticisms of FIP, QERA and xFIP is that they don't do enough to address batted ball tendencies of pitchers. In an effort to add more batted ball data into ERA prediction, Matthew Carruth and Graham MacAree, owners of StatCorner.com, developed tRA (which unofficially stands for true run average). The tRA metric yields an estimate of the number of runs per nine innings a pitcher should have allowed given his K, BB, HBP, HR and batted ball type rates (GB%, FB%, LD%, IFFB%).

Out values for the tRA statistic are assigned to each event according to how frequently each event results in an out. For example, a strikeout is virtually always an out so it has an out value of 1.000; a walk is never an out so it has an out value of 0.000; a line drive is an out about 26.4% of the time so it has an out value of 0.264. In addition, adjustments are made to out values for outs made on the bases such as ground ball double plays.

Each event is also assigned a run value which represents the absolute number of runs produced by each batted ball type in 2006. These values are based on a run expectancy matrix similar to Figure 25 of Chapter 5. Figure 51 gives out and run values for the 2006 season. For example, a line drive was worth 0.391 runs on average.

Figure 51: tRA Out and Run Values by Batted Ball Type, 2006

Event	Out	Run
K	1.000	-0.113
IFF	0.971	-0.088
OFF (exc. HR)	0.867	0.028
GB	0.808	0.045
LD	0.264	0.391
HBP	0.000	0.355
BB	0.000	0.355
HR	0.000	1.409

Source: StatCorner.com

In order to compute the out and run values, Carruth and MacAree used Retrosheet.org data for 2003-2006 and MLB.com play by play data for 2007-2009.

The out values for all the batters faced by a pitcher in a season are summed to get expected outs. Similarly, all the run values are summed to get expected runs allowed. Then expected outs and expected runs are plugged into the following formula to get tRA or expected runs per 9 innings:

$$tRA = (\text{Expected runs/Expected outs}) \times 27$$

For example, Blanton allowed 283 ground balls in 2005. Applying the 2006 out and run values (which should be very close to the 2005 values), we would assume that each of his ground balls was worth .808 outs. Consequently, his expected number of outs on ground balls was 283 x 0.808 = 228.7. Similarly, Blanton would have been expected to allow 283 x .045 = 12.7 runs due to ground balls. These same calculations would be done for each event (K, IFF, OFF, LD, HBP, BB and HR). Summing the results for outs and runs respectively yields 584 expected outs and 108 expected runs. His resulting tRA was (108/584) x 27 = 4.99.

Since roughly 92% of all runs are earned, one can convert tRA to the ERA scale (tERA) by multiplying by 0.92. Blanton's tERA of 4.59 was much higher than his actual ERA of 3.53.

While tRA was shown by Wyers to be a better predictor of future ERA than either ERA or FIP, there is no evidence that it works better than xFIP or QERA. Also, bear in mind that none of these component-based ERAs (FIP, QERA, xFIP or tRA) are highly accurate predictors of ERA.

A critique of tRA is that some of its components – particularly line drive and home run rates – tend to fluctuate wildly from year-to-year and can regress to the mean after extreme years. The concept of regression to the mean refers to the tendency of a pitcher with a very high or low LD% (or some other statistic) in a given year to be closer to the league average in that statistic in the following year.

In order to correct for regression to the mean, Carruth and MacAree developed a more complex version of tRA called tRA*. They moved each component of tRA (K%, IFF% , OFF% GB%, LD%, HBP%, BB%, HR%) closer to league averages before computing tRA*. The adjustment was based on the number of batters a pitcher faced and the year to year correlation of the particular statistic. The resulting tRA* statistic gives a little better estimate of pitcher's true talent level based on the statistics for a given year than tRA.

LEFT-ON-BASE PERCENTAGE

One factor that statistics such as FIP, xFIP and tRA ignore is a pitcher's ability to leave runners on base. As mentioned in Chapter 8, stranding runners is more a random event than a true skill for most pitchers. To measure the extent to which pitchers do prevent runners on base from scoring, Ron Shandler created the strand rate statistic which is the percentage of baserunners who fail to score.

Studenmund developed a similar statistic called left-on-base percentage (LOB%). LOB% is the number of baserunners who did not score divided by the total number of baserunners excluding those who scored on home runs. It is calculated as follows:

$$LOB\% = (H + BB + HBP - R)/(H + BB + HBP - (1.4 \times HR)).$$

LOB% can be found for all pitches in all seasons since 1974 at FanGraphs.com. The median LOB% for starting pitchers is about 72%. An LOB% of 75% or better is very good and an LOB% of less than 68% is sub-par. It is important to note that, while some pitchers are a little better at stranding runners than others, a very low or high LOB% for a pitcher in a given year is probably an indication of luck. Pitchers with extreme LOB% values are candidates to regress to the mean in succeeding years.

RUN PREVENTING EVENTS

The final statistic of this chapter is my own creation – run preventing events percentage (RPE%). Excluding bunts, an at bat can result in any of the following events:

1. K
2. BB
3. HBP
4. GB
5. LD
6. OFF
7. IFF

Based on Figures 49 and 51, three of the above events are generally favorable for pitchers and I call these run preventing events (RPE).

1. K
2. GB
3. IFF

A ground ball is not as easy an out as a strikeout or an infield fly, and can have a negative result for a pitcher. However, a high GB rate will generally help a pitcher prevent runs over the course of a season. On the other hand, it is generally good for pitchers to avoid the following events:

1. BB
2. HBP
3. LD
4. OFF

Run Preventing Event Percentage (RPE%) is the proportion of batters facing a pitcher that result in strikeouts, ground balls or infield flies:

$$RPE\% = (K + GB + IFF)/BFP$$

The 2008 National League RPE% leaders are listed in Figure 52. While RPE% does not have the same accuracy as a statistic such as tRA, which applies different weights to different events, there is value in its simplicity.

Figure 52: Run Preventing Event Percentage Leaders in National League, 2008

Pitcher	BFP	SO	GB	IFF	RPE	RPE%
Brandon Webb	944	183	439	8	630	.667
Derek Lowe	851	147	397	9	553	.649
Tim Hudson	573	85	265	6	356	.621
CC Sabathia	516	128	182	8	318	.616
Aaron Cook	886	96	413	22	.531	.599

Data from FanGraphs.com

PERCENTILES

Figure 53 shows the percentiles for some of the statistics in this chapter for MLB starters in 2008. For example, it reveals that a typical GB% is 43.5, 36.1 is very low and 51.5 is very high. Some of the component-based ERAs (FIP, xFIP and QERA) are excluded because they are on the same scale as ERA and should be interpreted similarly.

Figure 53: Percentiles for Fielding Independent Pitching in MLB, 2008

Percentile	ERA	GB%	RPE%	tRA	LOB%
Best	1.65	64.2	66.7	2.38	0.83
90%	3.21	51.5	57.3	3.54	0.77
75%	3.68	48.2	55.0	3.93	0.75
50%	4.22	43.5	52.3	4.59	0.72
25%	5.07	39.3	48.5	5.33	0.68
10%	5.85	36.1	45.4	5.97	0.65
Worst	6.75	21.7	41.9	7.03	0.60

Data from FanGraphs.com, StatCorner.com

WHICH STATISTICS SHOULD WE BE USING?

Before moving on to a new section, now is a good time to step back and talk about which pitching statistics fans should be using. First, I advise that one look at a variety of statistics rather than relying too heavily on one measure. Despite its limitations, there is no need to abandon ERA in evaluation of past performance. A pitcher's responsibility is to prevent the opposition from scoring runs and ERA does a reasonably good job of measuring how well a pitcher has done that in most cases. However, ERA should be viewed in combination with peripheral statistics which are more independent of a pitcher's teammates. The preferred peripheral statistics of many performance analysts are K/9, BB/9 and GB%. As detailed in Chapter 8, win/loss record for individual pitchers should generally be avoided because it is too dependent on events beyond a pitcher's control to be reliable for pitcher evaluation.

While the ERA statistic works reasonably well for assessment of past performance, it is influenced by events that are at least somewhat beyond a pitcher's control and is not the best measure of true talent. Component-based ERAs such as FIP, xFIP, QERA and tRA are better indicators of true talent and do a little better job than current ERA of projecting future ERA. BABIP is a good tool for identifying which pitchers may have been fortunate or unfortunate in the past year and which pitchers may improve or regress in the coming year. These measures should not be used as replacements for ERA. Instead, they should be used in conjunction with ERA to give a more complete picture of a pitcher's past and potential future performance.

Chapter 10

Relief Pitching

No part of the game has changed as much in the past few decades as relief pitching. Starters are pitching fewer innings and relief staffs are getting more work with each decade. At the same time, the roles of relievers are becoming increasingly specialized. Most fans realize that relief pitching has become an important part of winning in today's game but reliever performance traditionally has not been measured well.

Evaluation of relief pitcher performance is a challenge for a few reasons. First, earned run average is not a very reliable statistic for evaluation of relievers because relievers often enter games with runners on base and give up another pitcher's runs. As a result, a bullpen hurler can have a relatively low ERA without actually being effective. Additionally, relievers pitch so few innings that their statistics can be influenced heavily by a couple of poor outings. Finally, the value of the innings that relievers pitch depends on game situations more than any other players and situational pitching is not accounted for by traditional measures.

PERIPHERALS FOR RELIEVERS

One solution to the ERA limitation for relievers is to evaluate relievers using the peripheral statistics introduced in Chapter 8: BB/9, K/9, K/BB, H/9, WHIP and HR/9. The percentiles for relievers with 40 or more appearances in 2008 are shown in Figure 54. These statistics yielded somewhat different results for relievers than starters. Relievers typically walked more batters per nine innings than starters (3.7 versus 3.1 on average). They also struck out more batters (7.8 versus 6.2), gave up fewer hits (8.1 versus 9.2), allowed fewer homers (0.81 versus 1.02) and had lower ERAs (3.63 versus 4.22).

Figure 54: Peripheral Statistic Percentiles for MLB Relievers, 2008

Percentile	ERA	BB/9	K/9	K/BB	H/9	WHIP	HR/9
Best	0.59	0.8	12.7	12.8	4.1	0.66	0.00
90%	2.24	2.4	10.3	3.7	6.3	1.03	0.39
75%	2.87	3.0	9.1	2.7	7.1	1.19	0.57
50%	3.63	3.7	7.8	2.1	8.1	1.36	0.81
25%	4.62	4.4	6.4	1.6	9.4	1.47	1.11
10%	5.28	5.4	5.6	1.4	10.5	1.62	1.56
Worst	8.46	7.0	2.9	0.8	12.9	2.10	2.84

Data from Baseball-Databank.org

SAVES

Peripheral statistics are limited by the fact that they do not consider the context that is so important to a reliever's work. As mentioned in Chapter 1, Jerome Holtzman invented the save statistic to account for the impact of game situations facing many relievers. A pitcher gets credit for a save when he finishes a game won by his club, is not the winning pitcher and either (a) enters the game with a lead of three runs or fewer and pitches at least one inning, (b) enters the game with the potential tying run on base, at bat, or on deck, or (c) pitches effectively for at least three innings.

We can be reasonably certain that a pitcher with a large number of saves finished off a lot of close games and this has value to a team. However, it is also important to consider the opportunities a pitcher had to achieve saves. This is accomplished by the save percentage statistic – the percentage of save opportunities which result in saves.

While the save statistic gives some context to a reliever's innings, some saves have quite a bit more impact than others. Suppose Boston Red Sox closer Jonathan Papelbon enters the game in the ninth inning with a three run lead and nobody on base. He proceeds to give up two runs but gets a save when right fielder J.D. Drew makes a diving catch with the potential winning run in scoring position. Papelbon does not pitch effectively in that inning but still gets credit for a save.

In another instance, New York Yankees closer Mariano Rivera comes into a game in the eighth inning with a one run lead and two men on base. He survives the eighth inning without allowing a run to score and then pitches a perfect ninth to preserve the victory. Each pitcher gets credit for a save but the save statistic does not account for the fact that Rivera inherits a more difficult situation and pitches more effectively than Papelbon. As shown in Figure 55, Los Angeles Angels closer Francisco Rodriguez led the MLB with 62 saves in 2008.

Figure 55: Saves Leaders in MLB, 2008

Pitcher	Saves
Francisco Rodriguez	62
Jose Valverde	44
Joakim Soria	42
Brad Lidge	41
Jonathan Papelbon	41
Brian Wilson	41

Source: Baseball-Reference.com

HOLDS

With the specialization of modern bullpens, one pitcher on each team – the closer – generally gets most of the save opportunities. However, other relievers besides closers also contribute to victories. The hold statistic helps to give situational pitching credit to relievers in roles other than closer. A relief pitcher gets credit for a hold if he enters a game in a save situation, records at least one out and leaves the game without giving up the lead. A pitcher does not get credit for a hold if he finishes the game, so it is impossible for a pitcher to get a save and a hold in the same game.

Like the save statistic, the hold statistic treats all opportunities equally. For example, a three-run lead with nobody on base counts the same as a one-run lead with the bases loaded. One of the biggest problems with both saves and holds is that a pitcher who enters a tie game, one of the most crucial situations of all, can get neither a hold nor a save. He can get a win in that scenario if his team scores while he is in the game, but he has little control over that. Figure 56 shows that Los Angeles Angels reliever Scot Shields led MLB with 31 holds in 2008.

Figure 56: Holds Leaders in MLB, 2008

Pitcher	Holds
Scot Shields	31
Carlos Marmol	30
Kyle McClellan	30
Dan Wheeler	26
Eddie Guardado	25
Rafael Perez	25
Damaso Marte	25

Source: Baseball-Reference.com

WIN PROBABILITY ADDED

In the Rivera/Papelbon example above, we saw that the save statistic did not account for the fact that Rivera entered the game in a more difficult situation and pitched much more effectively than Papelbon. The win probability added statistic, introduced in Chapter 6 for hitters, gives relievers credit based on the effect each batter faced has on the team's probability of winning. These probabilities vary depending on the game state before and after each play.

As mentioned in Chapter 6, Eldon and Harlan Mills applied Player Win Averages – an early version of WPA – to the 1969 season using play-by-play data purchased from the Elias Sports Bureau. One interesting result was that the leading pitchers in player win average were relievers Tug McGraw of the New York Mets and Ken Tatum of the California Angels. This was noteworthy at the time, as relievers were not valued by fans and media in 1969 as much as they are today.

The calculation of WPA for relievers is essentially the same as that for batters. Suppose Tigers reliever Bobby Seay comes into the game in the top of the eighth with a two run lead, no outs and a runner on first. There is a 0.837 (83.7%) expectancy that an average team will win a game given that situation. Now, assume that Seay strikes out the first batter. There is now one out and the probability of winning increases to 0.884 (88.4%). Subtracting the win expectation before the strikeout from the win expectation after the strikeout gives us the value of the play in terms of the probability of winning added by the strikeout, that is, 0.047 (0.884 – 0.837) or 4.7%.

Finally, suppose the next batter, facing Seay, doubles home a run. That gives the Tigers a one run lead with a runner on second and one out. The probability of winning goes down to 0.774 so

Seay loses .110 (0.774 – 0.884) points on that batter.

Summing all the gains and subtracting all the losses for all the batters Seay faces during a season yields his WPA. WPA is especially useful for relievers, because of the impact their innings typically have on the outcomes of games. Figure 57 below shows that the top relievers in terms of WPA in 2008 included a mix of closers, set-up men and other pitchers. It includes some different names from the lists of saves and holds leaders in Figures 55 and 56.

Figure 57: Top WPA for MLB Relievers, 2008

Pitcher	IP	WPA	Saves	Holds
Brad Lidge	69.1	5.37	41	0
Mariano Rivera	70.2	4.47	39	0
Joakim Soria	67.1	4.08	42	0
Carlos Marmol	87.1	3.77	7	30
Bobby Jenks	61.2	3.47	30	0
Francisco Rodriguez	68.1	3.33	62	0
J.P.Howell	89.1	3.33	3	14
Joe Nathan	67.2	3.26	39	0
Brad Ziegler	59.2	3.20	11	9
Ron Mahay	64.2	2.83	0	21
Damaso Marte	65.0	2.83	5	25
Grant Balfour	58.1	2.69	4	14
Eddie Guardado	56.1	2.52	4	25
Scott Downs	70.2	2.51	5	24
Brian Fuentes	62.2	2.21	30	6

Sources: Baseball-Reference.com, FanGraphs.com

LEVERAGE INDEX

Which pitchers typically worked in the most pressing situations? This can be answered using the leverage index concept developed by Tom Tango. Leverage index (LI) measures how critical a given plate appearance is in determining the final result of a game by looking at the difference in win probability between the best and worst case scenarios. For example, suppose Minnesota Twins reliever Matt Guerrier enters a game in which the Twins have a nine-run lead with nobody on base in the ninth inning. In that situation, there is little difference between giving up a home run and getting the batter out on the probability of winning the game. This is an example of a low-leverage situation. However, if Guerrier comes into a game with two on with nobody out and a one-run lead in the ninth inning, then allowing a home run will be much more damaging than getting the batter out. That is a high-leverage situation.

Tango assigns a value of one to an average game situation. Higher-leverage situations have values of more than one and lower-leverage situations have values less than one. Each game scenario is then given a leverage index relative to the average situation. A leverage index of two, for example, means that the given at bat has twice as much impact on the outcome of the game as the average at bat. Leverage indexes are averaged over the batters faced by a pitcher to arrive at leverage index per plate appearance (pLI). Not surprisingly, Figure 58 shows that the top five relievers in pLI in 2008 were closers.

Figure 58: Leverage Index Leaders in MLB, 2008

Pitcher	IP	pLI
Francisco Rodriguez	68.1	2.54
Brian Wilson	62.1	2.25
B.J. Ryan	58.0	2.19
Kevin Gregg	68.2	2.13
George Sherrill	53.1	2.02

Source: FanGraphs.com

WRAP-UP

In conclusion, evaluation of relievers is tricky, but there are new tools available which give us a more complete assessment than traditional measures. There is no reason to abandon statistics such as ERA, strikeout rate, walk rate, holds and saves in evaluating relievers. However, statistics such as WPA and pLI enrich the evaluation of reliever performance by considering the context in which relievers pitched.

Remember that many of the measures we have covered in the last three chapters attempted to isolate pitching from fielding. We have yet to delve into the fielding part of the run prevention equation. That will be the topic of the next three chapters.

Illustration by Samara Pearlstein

Chapter 11

Individual Fielding

If you have spent any time on the Internet visiting various baseball sites, you have probably read something about the Derek Jeter fielding controversy. The national media has raved about the New York Yankees shortstop's fielding prowess for years, and managers and coaches gave him three Gold Glove awards from 2004-2006. However, modern sabermetric analysis suggests that Jeter was not a very good fielder during that period. In fact, many performance analysts rated the Yankee's shortstop as a below-average defender from 2004-2006 and as the worst shortstop in baseball in 2007. In this chapter, we will discuss the methods which led them to those conclusions.

FIELDING PERCENTAGE

Historically, the most commonly reported fielding measure has been fielding percentage (FPCT) which is the proportion of a fielder's total plays – putouts (PO), assists (A) and errors (E) – that result in a putout or an assist. It is calculated as follows:

$$\text{total plays} = PO + A + E$$

$$FPCT = (\text{total plays} - E)/\text{total plays}$$

For example, Jeter had a .970 FPCT in 2007, which means that he recorded a putout or an assist on 97% of his plays and made an error on 3% of his plays.

Avoiding errors is a positive thing so FPCT has some value, but it also has some important flaws. One problem is that error totals are influenced by the subjectivity of official scorers. An official scorer is a hired employee of the home team, which means that there is potential for favoritism. A scorer might occasionally give the home team's fielders and hitters the benefit of the doubt by awarding hits on plays that might be called errors by another scorer. Over the course of a season, this could potentially influence a player's FPCT.

Even if we assume that there is no scorer bias and that all scorers judge plays the same way, FPCT is still fundamentally flawed. The problem is that it only penalizes a fielder for errors made and does not charge him for balls that he could not reach. For example, suppose that 100 balls are hit near Eddie Steady and the same 100 balls are hit near Rico Range. Let's say that Eddie makes zero errors on those plays and that Rico makes five errors. Also assume that Eddie converts 60 of those balls into outs and Rico converts 80 into outs. Which one is the better fielder on those 100 plays?

If we use FPCT as our measure of a player's fielding contribution, then Eddie (1.000) is considered to be the superior fielder to Rico (.941) by a wide margin. However, FPCT does not account for the 20 additional plays which Rico makes. Failing to reach a ball has essentially the same effect as making an error: a batter reaches base and no out is recorded. Yet, FPCT does not penalize Eddie for his failure to make 20 plays and does not give Rico credit for his superior range. A more fair way to assess the fielding performance of Eddie and Rico would be to consider that Eddie converted 60 of the 100 batted balls into outs while Rico converted 80 of 100. That is the basis of the more sophisticated fielding measures covered below.

RANGE FACTOR

The range factor (RF) statistic was originated by a Philadelphia scorer in 1872 and was re-introduced a century later by Bill James in 1977. The basic RF formula is:

$$RF = ((PO + A) / Inn) \times 9$$

In words, RF is the average number of successful plays that a fielder makes per nine innings. RF is an improvement over FPCT because it punishes a player for plays not made as well as misplays. In 2007, Jeter had a RF of 4.0, which means that he made four plays per nine innings. That ranked him 27th among 29 MLB shortstops with at least 700 innings played.

The problem with RF is that it can be influenced as much by the make-up of a team as it is by the skill of a particular fielder. For example, an outfielder playing behind a predominantly ground ball pitching staff will have fewer opportunities to make putouts than an outfielder on a staff of fly ball pitchers. Similarly, the opportunities of all fielders on a team will be reduced if the team's pitchers strike out a large number of batters. Our goal is to evaluate the fielding of a player independent of his pitching staff and other teammates and RF does not always do that effectively.

ADJUSTED RANGE FACTOR

In order to address some of the shortcomings of simple RF, analyst Tom Tippett developed the adjusted range factor statistic in the late 1980s. In his system, he removed plays that have nothing to do with physical range, such as taking a throw at first base or making the pivot on a double play. He also made adjustments for team factors such as strikeouts, ground ball/fly ball tendencies of pitching staffs and handedness of pitchers and opposing batters.

We implied in the discussion of simple RF why it is important to adjust for strikeout and ground ball/fly ball rates of pitching staffs in measuring range. The handedness of opposing batters is also a factor as batters tend to pull the ball more often than they hit the ball to the opposite field. Thus, we would expect a team that faces a lot of right-handed batters to have more balls hit to the left side. It is also important to adjust for handedness of pitchers on a fielder's team because that also affects the location of batted balls. For example, a heavily left-handed staff will face more right-handed batters and thus tend to see more balls hit to the left side. Adjusted RF takes all of these factors into account, which makes it a better measure of a fielder's range than simple RF.

For more information on adjusted RF, you can consult Tippett's article at Diamond-Mind.com (diamond-mind.com/articles/defeval.htm)

One item for which the adjusted RF does not adjust is the actual location of batted balls. Location is a key factor in most of the rest of the defensive statistics introduced in this chapter.

ZONE RATING

When he was working at STATS in the late 1980s, John Dewan incorporated location of batted balls into the measurement of range with his zone rating (ZR) statistic. Zone rating allows us to evaluate a fielder based on his opportunities to make plays as well as how many plays he makes. The results from this system were first published in the 1990 *STATS Baseball Scoreboard*.

In computing ZR, STATS divides the baseball field into small sections and assigns these sections to fielders based on batted ball location data. If half the balls hit into a certain area are converted into outs by all the players in MLB at a given position, then that area is considered to be part of the zone for that position. For example, if 1,000 ground balls are hit into area X and 506 are converted into outs by baseball's shortstops, then Area X is considered to be part of the zone of responsibility for the shortstop position.

The calculation of ZR for a given player considers three factors: The number of balls hit into his zone while he is in the game (balls in zone), the number of balls in the zone that he converts into outs (plays made in zone) and the number of plays outside his zone that he converts to outs (plays made outside of zone). ZR is computed as follows:

$$\text{total plays made} = \text{plays made in zone} + \text{plays made outside of zone}$$

$$ZR = (\text{total plays made})/(\text{balls in zone} + \text{plays made outside of zone})$$

Simply stated, ZR is the percentage of balls in a player's zone that he converts into outs plus extra credit for plays he makes outside his zone. A common misconception is that ZR gives a player credit for getting to a ball even if he makes a throwing error. In actuality, a player only gets credit for making a play if an out is recorded. Thus, he would not get credit for fielding a ball cleanly if he failed to get the runner out due to a throwing error.

Jeter's .765 ZR in 2007 tells us that he converted 76.5% of his opportunities to make plays into outs. That was the second worst in MLB to Tampa Bay Rays shortstop Brendan Harris.

While ZR is an improvement over RF, it is still flawed. Let's say that Shortstop A has 400 balls hit into his zone, converts 350 into outs, and also makes 40 plays outside his zone. Next, assume that Shortstop B has 400 balls hit into his zone, converts 370 into outs and makes 20 plays outside his zone. The zone ratings for these shortstops are calculated below:

$$\text{Shortstop A: } ZR = (350 + 40)/(400 + 40) = .886$$

$$\text{Shortstop B: } ZR = (370 + 20)/(400 + 20) = .929$$

Both shortstops have the same number of in zone opportunities (400) and make the same number of plays (390) but shortstop B has a significantly higher ZR. This example shows that if a relatively large proportion of a fielder's successful plays are out of zone plays, then he may be undervalued by ZR. Such a scenario may sometimes be due to player positioning. The ZR statistic assumes that a player is positioned in the middle of his zone at the beginning of a play. If a player is frequently positioned outside the zone or at the edge of the zone before a play starts, then he will make more out of zone plays but will also make fewer in zone plays similar to Player A. The ZR formula unfairly penalizes such a player by adding his out of zone plays to his number of opportunities.

REVISED ZONE RATING

After Dewan left STATS and founded Baseball Info Solutions (BIS) in 2002, he addressed the above limitation of the zone rating statistic by developing the revised zone rating metrics. The revised zone rating metrics separate the plays a player made inside his zone from the plays he made outside the zone.

Another difference between the two systems is that revised zone rating does not give a player extra credit for having both an assist and a putout on a double play. The ability to turn double plays is a valuable skill but Dewan's feeling was that a statistic, with the primary purpose of measuring range, should not credit two plays to a player that really made one. The final difference between the two methods is the company collecting the data. Zone rating is based on STATS data and revised zone rating is based on data from Baseball Info Solutions (BIS). Thus, there may be small differences between the two systems in the determination of zones. The revised zone rating system is comprised of the following measures:

1. Balls in play within a fielder's zone (BIZ)
2. Plays made in the zone (PLAYS)
3. Percentage of balls in zone converted into outs (RZR)
4. Plays made outside the zone (OOZ)

Figure 59 shows that San Francisco Giants shortstop Omar Vizquel converted 350 of 395 (86%) of balls in his zone into outs in 2007. Jack Wilson of the Pittsburgh Pirates had a similar number of balls hit into his zone (396) but had a smaller RZR (81.6%). Conversely, Vizquel made fewer out of zone plays (47) than Wilson (76). These data suggest that Vizquel was the steadier fielder on balls hit in the shortstop zone but Wilson was perhaps better at making more difficult plays.

Figure 59: Revised Zone Rating Statistics for Omar Vizquel and Jack Wilson, 2007

Player	BIZ	PLAYS	RZR	OOZ
Omar Vizquel	395	350	.886	47
Jack Wilson	396	323	.816	76

Source: The Fielding Bible, 2009, pg. 355

While ZR and the revised zone rating measures are regarded by most analysts as more accurate than RF, they do have limitations. First, they are dependent on the reliability of those collecting the data. The scorers need to judge whether balls are actually hit into a zone and have to distinguish between fly balls and line drives as there is a different zone for each.

A second concern is that ZR and revised zone rating treat all balls in a zone the same even though it may be more difficult for a fielder to reach some balls within the zone than others. Ideally, a player should get more credit for making a difficult play that most fielders do not make than for a routine play. Finally, ZR and revised zone rating fail to take additional factors into consideration such as ballpark dimensions and how hard the ball was hit.

PLAY-BY-PLAY SYSTEMS

New Systems have been developed to address some of the limitations of ZR and revised zone rating. They include:

1. Plus/minus system (+/-)
2. Defensive runs saved (DRS)
3. Ultimate zone rating (UZR)
4. Probabilistic model of range (PMR)

All four systems use detailed play-by-play data on location and type of batted ball from BIS. The methods are similar in theory but use somewhat different algorithms and thus produce varying results for some players.

BIS video scouts watch videotape of every MLB game and every play is entered into a database which includes exact direction, distance, speed and type of every batted ball. Direction and distance are entered by simply recording the exact location of the ball on a replica of the field shown on the computer screen. The speed of a batted ball is recorded as soft, medium and hard. Each play is also categorized according to batted ball type: groundball, line drive, fly ball, fliner (a cross between a fly ball and a line drive) or bunt.

PLUS/MINUS SYSTEM

In 1999, Dewan developed an ultimate zone rating statistic (not the same ultimate zone rating used today) using data on location and batted ball type to determine how many plays each fielder made compared to the average fielder at his position. He published the results in The 2000 *STATS Baseball Scoreboard*. After leaving STATS and founding BIS in 2002, Dewan produced the more sophisticated plus/minus system to evaluate fielders. He first published the plus/minus methodology and results in *The Fielding Bible* in 2006 and added enhancements in the *The Fielding Bible – Volume II* in 2009.

The plus/minus system breaks the field into small areas and determines the probabilities of players making plays in each area based on location, speed (hard, medium, soft) and batted ball type (ground ball, fly ball, line drive, bunt). The plus/minus system uses these probabilities to determine how many outs each player was expected to make and how many he actually did make in comparison to the average player.

Dewan explains that each type of play (e.g. softly hit ground ball hit into the hole between short and third) has a difficulty determined by how many times all fielders in MLB converted that play into an out. For example, if that play was made 30% of the time, then a player gets a score of +0.70 for making that play. If he doesn't make that play, then he gets a -0.30 score.

The scores on all of a player's plays are summed to compute his +/- rating. This rating represents how many plays the player made above or below the number of plays an average player at his position would make given the same opportunities. For example, Jeter had a +/- of -34 in 2007 indicating that he made 34 plays fewer than the average shortstop would have been expected to make given the same opportunities. Complete results for all years since 2004 can be found at BillJamesOnline.net.

Dewan converts plays made above average to defensive runs above average using situational run expectancies similar to those described in Chapter 5. Based on these expectancies, Dewan determined that each plus/minus point for a shortstop is worth 0.76 runs. For example, Jeter cost his team 34 x 0.76 = 26 runs in comparison to the average shortstop. For outfielders and corner infielders, Dewan adjusts the +/- figure for the potential of individual balls going for extra bases. He calls this enhanced plus/minus.

DEFENSIVE RUNS SAVED

Dewan also introduced defensive runs saved (DRS) in *The Fielding Bible – Volume II*. DRS is an extension of the plus/minus system. In addition to +/- runs saved, DRS includes other sources of runs saved by position:

1. Runs saved on bunts for corner infielders

2. Double plays for 2B/SS/3B

3. Arm runs saved

4. Home run runs saved for outfielders

For example, Jeter had -26 plus/minus runs and +3 double play runs for a total of -23 DRS in 2007. Complete DRS data can be found on BillJamesOnline.com.

ULTIMATE ZONE RATING

Inspired by Dewan's original ultimate zone rating statistic presented in *The 2000 STATS Baseball Scoreboard*, Mitchel Lichtman developed a more comprehensive version of ultimate zone rating (UZR), which he introduced in 2003. While Dewan's plus/minus and Lichtman's UZR systems were developed independently, both creators report that the basic methodologies are similar.

Lichtman, who has done statistical analysis for MLB teams, explains that UZR is an extension of simple ZR. First, the field is broken into 78 zones, 64 of which are used in calculating UZR. Suppose the average shortstop turns 75% of all balls hit into zone X into outs. Then assume that

Jeter turns 70% of plays made in zone X to outs. This means that Jeter makes 5% fewer plays in zone X than the average shortstop. Now suppose there are 100 balls hit into zone X while Jeter is on the field. Since 5% of 100 is 5, this means that Jeter is 5 plays below what would be expected from the average shortstop in zone X.

Lichtman converts plays above/below average into runs saved/cost using the linear weights methodology introduced in Chapter 5. These run estimates are based on the number of hits in each zone and the average run value of hits in these zones. Suppose that a play made by a shortstop in zone X is worth 0.80 runs. This means that Jeter is 5 x 0.80 = 4 runs below average in that zone.

If we repeat the above process for each zone on the field and sum the results, we obtain Jeter's unadjusted UZR. However, Lichtman also adjusts for factors beyond location which influence a fielder's ability to turn batted balls into outs. Like the plus/minus system, UZR considers type of batted ball, how hard the ball was hit and the ballpark in determining the difficulty of the play in each zone. In addition, UZR also considers the following:

1. Handedness of the pitcher

2. Handedness of the batter

3. Groundball/fly ball ratio of the pitcher

4. Base/out state (e.g. An infielder may be playing in with a runner on third with less than two outs.)

Adjusting for all of these factors in each zone before summing the results yields a fielder's UZR. For example, Jeter had a -15.3 UZR in 2007. This indicates that he cost his team 15.3 more runs with his fielding than would have been expected by the average shortstop in the same opportunities.

Lichtman originally used the STATS data to calculate UZR but now calculates UZR separately for STATS and BIS data. The results produced by the BIS system can be found at FanGraphs.com for all seasons back to 2002. Included are the following UZR statistics for each fielder in each season:

1. Range runs (RngR) – runs saved/cost by a player above/below an average fielder based on his ability to reach and convert into an out balls hit anywhere on the field, compared to an average fielder at his position.

2. Error runs (ErrR) – runs saved/cost by a player above/below an average fielder based on his ability to avoid errors. This includes all types of errors including fielding errors, throwing errors and errors made catching throws from other fielders.

3. Double play runs (DPR) – runs saved/cost by a player above/below average based on his ability to turn double plays. This includes the fielder starting a double play and the player making the pivot.

4. Outfield arm runs (ARM) – runs saved/cost based on an outfielder's ability to throw runners out and to prevent runners from advancing. Outfield arm ratings will be discussed in more detail in the outfielder throwing arms section below.

5. Total runs above average (UZR) = RngR + ErrR + DPR + ARM (for outfielders).

6. Ultimate zone rate per 150 games (UZR/150) – runs saved/cost per 150 defensive games.

One reason error runs are calculated separately from range runs is that the average error is slightly more damaging in terms of potential run cost than the average ball that simply gets by the reach of a fielder. Specifically, a throwing error by a middle infielder may result in a two-base error whereas a ball that gets beyond his reach will probably just be a single.

More importantly, we have more information about errors than hits. Suppose the same ball (batted ball type, location, speed, etc) is hit on two occasions and one is called a hit and one is called an error. On the ball called a hit, a fielder is penalized based on how often the same ball is successfully fielded by an average fielder (e.g. 40%). While a hit may or may not have been an easy play in reality, errors are known to be plays that a fielder should have made about 98% of the time. Thus, a player is usually penalized more in this system for making an error than for allowing a hit because we know the error was a relatively easy play.

Jeter had the following numbers in 2007: -16.0 RngR, -0.4 Error Runs (ErrR) and 1.1 DPR. Summing those figures yields a -15.3 UZR, which indicates that he cost his team 15.3 more runs with his fielding than would have been expected by the average shortstop. The UZR/150 statistic helps to compare players with different amounts of playing time. Jeter's UZR/150 of -16.7 indicates that he was 16.7 runs per 150 games worse than the average shortstop.

PROBABILISTIC MODEL OF RANGE

The Probabilistic Model of Range system was created by David Pinto. Like +/- and UZR, PMR measures range based on the difficulty in fielding a play with more challenging plays carrying greater weight in determining a fielder's range. Pinto uses balls in play data from BIS for all games in a given year to establish the difficulty of plays and thus the probability of making an out. Six factors are used to calculate the probability of turning a batted ball into an out:

1. Batted ball type (ground ball, line drive, fly ball)

2. How hard a ball was hit (hard, medium, soft)

3. Direction

4. Handedness of batter

5. Handedness of pitcher

6. Ballpark (e.g. the small left field at Fenway Park and large left field at Coors Field influence probabilities for left fielders in those parks.)

Pinto then determines, for each fielder, how many balls were in play when he was on the field, how many he should have been expected to turn into outs and how many he actually turned into outs. The idea is that good fielders will record more outs than expected and poor fielders will record fewer outs than expected.

For example, 4,117 balls were in play when Jeter was on the field in 2007. Based on the six parameters listed above and data for all fielders, it was determined that Jeter should have turned approximately 462 balls into outs. In actuality, he turned 421 balls into outs so he made 41 fewer plays than would be expected by the average shortstop. That number is called Plays Made Above Average (PMAA). Pinto has not yet converted his PMR system into runs but one can apply Dewan's 0.76 factor to Jeter to get an estimate: -41 x 0.76 = -31 runs below average.

Pinto also ranks players according to ratio of outs to predicted outs:

$$Ratio = (outs/predicted\ outs) \times 100$$

A ratio of 100 is average, more than 100 is above average and less than 100 is below average. For example, Jeter's had 421 outs and 462 predicted outs yielding a ratio of 91. This means that he made 9% fewer plays than would have been expected by the average shortstop. Pinto publishes the PMR statistics annually at BaseballMusings.com.

TOTAL ZONE

Data for direct observation systems such as plus/minus, UZR and PMR are only available back to 2002. In order to evaluate players in prior years, a less complex method and potentially less accurate method has to be used. Analyst Sean Smith used the Retrosheet.org play-by-play database to develop his total zone system covering seasons as far back as 1954. Total zone considers the following items:

1. Plays made
2. Errors
3. Which fielder makes each out
4. Batted ball type (when available)
5. Which fielder fielded each hit (1989-1999 and 2003-2009)
6. Handedness of pitcher and batter
7. Park adjustments
8. Zone data when available (1989-1999)

Smith calculates plays made above average and converts that into runs saved using situational run expectancies. The resulting statistic is called total zone fielding runs above average (Rtz). According to Rtz, Jeter cost his team 15.8 runs in comparison to the average shortstop in 2007. The Rtz statistic data can be found at Baseball-Reference.com.

Smith reports that the results yielded by his total zone system are comparable to those for the direct observation systems for years 2003 and forward. The statistics for earlier years probably produce somewhat less reliable results due to incomplete data. Still, it is believed by many analysts to be the best system for evaluating player fielding from 1954-2001.

POSITIONING

One common criticism of systems such as plus/minus, UZR and PMR is that they don't consider the positioning of fielders. Critics argue that a player with below-average physical range might make up for it with good positioning. While it is true that these systems do not consider positioning, this is not necessarily a problem in the evaluation of fielders. The purpose of these systems is not to measure physical range, but to determine how frequently players turned batted balls into outs. One shortstop might make plays because he has great physical range (the amount of ground he can cover). Another might make plays because he is a smart player who positions himself well. In theory, both types of fielders will be rewarded under these systems as they both will turn a large number of batted balls into outs. The range measured by these systems is actually a combination of physical range and positioning.

REPEATABILITY OF FIELDING DATA

Some fans have questioned the reliability of fielding statistics versus hitting and pitching statistics. It is true that a statistic such as UZR is not as reliable as the most repeatable hitting statistics (See Chapter 3). For example, UZR has a lower year to year correlation than on-base percentage (0.50 versus 0.67). However, UZR is more repeatable than commonly used statistics such as batting average (0.43) and ERA (0.33) and almost as repeatable as FIP (0.54). So, I would recommend using multiple years of data in assessing a player's inherent fielding ability, but I would say the same about many hitting and pitching measures.

USING MULTIPLE SYSTEMS TO EVALUATE PLAYERS

Another concern about fielding statistics is that a player's runs above/below average can vary significantly across systems even in the same year. This is because the systems use different algorithms and, in some cases, different databases. For this reason, I would not recommend using any one system as the end all of fielding evaluation. Ideally, one would look at more than one system over multiple years to get a better idea of how much a player contributed defensively. In general, the best fielders should rate well on all systems and the worst fielders should do poorly on all systems. However, some players do well by some methods and not so well by others. When this happens, it is probably an indication that these players fall somewhere between very good and very bad.

DISAGREEMENTS BETWEEN SYSTEMS

Figure 60 shows the runs saved by selected shortstops in 2007 according to four advanced fielding statistics detailed above:

1. +/-

2. UZR

3. PMR

4. Rtz

Sometimes these measures vary significantly for the same player. The figure shows that Jeter was below average on each system but was further below average on PMR (-31) and +/- (-26) than he was on UZR (-15) and Rtz (-16). Some analysts believe that when one system gives a higher/lower runs saved value than other systems, it might be over/under estimating the runs saved by that player. Based on that, I constructed an average range score (ARS) which averages the results over these four systems. The ARS gives us a conservative runs saved above average estimate for a player which alleviates the effect of one system perhaps over-valuing or under-valuing a player. For example, Jeter had an ARS of -22 runs below average in 2007, which falls between the extremes of -15 and -31.

Figure 60: Advanced Range Statistics for Selected MLB Shortstops, 2007

Player	Innings	UZR	+/-	PMR	Rtz	ARS
Derek Jeter	1,318	-15	-26	-31	-16	-22
Felipe Lopez	927	-9	-10	-14	-6	-10
Troy Tulowitzki	1,375	+15	+27	+38	+18	+24
Tony Pena	1,273	+17	+14	+24	+7	+16
Jhonny Peralta	1,348	-9	-2	+8	-6	-2

Data from FanGraphs.com, FieldingBible.com, BaseballMusings.com, BaseballProjection.com

Figure 60 illustrates that Colorado Rockies rookie Troy Tulowitzki and Kansas City Royals freshman Tony Pena, did well on every system. This gives us confidence that they both had excellent range in 2007. Players such as Jeter and Felipe Lopez of the Washington Nationals rated below average on every system, which suggests that they had poor range that year.

On the other hand, Cleveland Indians shortstop Jhonny Peralta (falling anywhere from -9 on UZR to +8 on PMR) was all over the place. Based on this, Peralta probably rated somewhere in between really good and really bad but we are less sure about his actual rank. For players with wildly varying runs saved estimates, we can look at past years and can also consider qualitative data to give us more confidence.

FANS' SCOUTING REPORT

Since fielding measures still do not work quite as well as hitting statistics, qualitative assessment of defense is valuable. One example of observation based evaluation is Tom Tango's Fans' Scouting Report. Tango annually conducts a survey on defensive skills where he asks fans to rate players based solely on observation and not to use any statistics or outside sources at all. Fans are instructed to scout players on reaction/instincts, acceleration/first few steps, speed, hands, release/footwork, throwing accuracy and throwing strength.

Tango then tabulates the survey results which can be seen in detail at TangoTiger.net. The results for our group of shortstops are shown in Figure 61 below. Tango explains that the league average rating for each of the seven categories is 50 and that a player with a rating of 70 or better is in the top 16% in MLB among all fielders without regard to position.

Figure 61: Fans' Scouting Report for Selected Shortstops, 2007

Player	Instincts	First step	Speed	Hands	Release	Arm strength	Accuracy	Total
Jeter	44	35	60	65	64	67	63	54
Lopez	41	53	63	30	34	56	31	45
Tulowitzki	79	77	68	86	89	90	94	82
Pena	64	73	60	67	66	68	53	66
Peralta	33	28	28	41	44	62	48	38

Source: TangoTiger.net

Figure 61 tells us that the fan scouting reports are in agreement with the statistical measures regarding Tulowitzki's fielding prowess. While Pena's 66 aggregate score did not rank him among the elite shortstops, he did receive above average scores from fans in most categories. Similarly, the fan data strengthen the argument that Lopez was a below average fielder in 2007. Jeter was ranked as an average fielder by fans but, interestingly, he had one of the lowest agreement scores (not shown). This means that there was much disagreement among fans on Jeter's fielding ability. Finally, Peralta – whose metrics varied substantially – was viewed by the fans as a below average defender.

OUTFIELDER THROWING ARMS

In order for an infielder to turn batted balls into outs, he must get to balls, field them cleanly and make good throws. As such, all of those items are included in the measurement of an infielder's range. Unlike an infielder, an outfielder does not need his arm to convert batted balls in the air to outs. Therefore, we evaluate his throwing arm separately from his range. While physical range may be the most important part of outfield defense, the ability to stop the running game by throwing runners out or preventing runner advancement is also very valuable. With that in mind, several analysts, including HardballTimes.com writer John Walsh, Sean Smith and Mitchel Lichtman, have developed statistics to evaluate outfielder arms.

Using the Retrosheet.org database, Walsh considers all situations where a runner has a chance to take an extra base on a ball hit to the outfield. This includes the following:

1. Single with runner on first base (second base unoccupied)

2. Double with runner on first base

3. Single with runner on second base

4. Fly out with runner on third base, fewer than two outs

5. Fly out with runner on second base, fewer than two outs (third base unoccupied)

For example, when a batter hits a single to left field with a runner on first and second base unoccupied, the runner either stops at second or attempts to advance to third. If the runner stops at second, then the outfielder would get credit for a hold. If the runner is thrown out at third, then the outfielder is credited with a kill.

For each outfielder, Walsh counts the numbers of advancement opportunities, holds and kills. He then determines how each outfielder compares to league average in both kills and holds. Finally, using situational run expectancies similar to those introduced in Chapter 5 (e.g. How likely is it for a run to score with a man on first and third and no outs compared to a runner on first and one out?), he then calculates runs saved above/below average for each outfielder. Other factors included in the calculation of runs saved are which fielder fielded the ball (e.g. a runner is more likely to go from first to third on a single to right than on a single to left) and the ballpark (e.g. it is a little easier for outfielder's to make plays on artificial turf because the ball gets to him more quickly).

For example, there were 149 opportunities for runners to take an extra base on Philadelphia Phillies outfielder Shane Victorino in 2008. Based on these opportunities and on run expectancies, Walsh determined that Victorino had a kill+ ratio of 111. This says that he was 11% above the average center fielder in throwing out baserunners. Similarly, his hold+ ratio (123) indicates that he was 23% above average at preventing advancement. Finally, Walsh estimated that Victorino prevented 6.7 runs above average per 200 opportunities (over approximately a full season) with his arm.

As he did with his total zone system, Smith developed another system for evaluating outfield arms using the same Retrosheet.org data he used for total zone. Smith calculates outfield arms runs saved above or below average (Rof) based on baserunner kills and advancement. The Rof measure can be found at BaseballProjection.org and Baseball-Reference.org. The systems of both Smith and Walsh work for all years since 1954. Since Retrosheet.org does not have as much detailed information on hits and batted ball types prior to 2003, the results on both systems (Walsh and Smith) are a little less reliable in those years.

As noted in the UZR section, Lichtman includes a similar system to Walsh and Smith for evaluating outfielder arms back to 2002. His outfielder arm statistic (ARM) is part of the UZR system described above and can be found at FanGraphs.com. Partly because the BIS system has more detailed data than Retrosheet.org, Lichtman adjusts for more factors than Walsh and Smith. In addition to all the items included in the two above systems, Lichtman also considers more specific batted ball location, the speed of the batter/ base runner and the batter frequency of singles, doubles and triples to each field.

WHAT ABOUT CATCHERS?

We have covered infield and outfield defense in depth in this chapter but we have yet to discuss the evaluation of catcher defense. The range statistics which have been the main focus of this chapter do not work well for catchers because physical range is not a large part of a catcher's job. We will cover catcher defense in Chapter 12.

Illustration by Samara Pearlstein

Chapter 12

Catcher Defense

The catching position is the most difficult to quantify defensively. Instead of the physical range characteristics cited for infielders and outfielders in Chapter 11, the handling of pitchers is believed by many insiders to be the most important defensive skill of any catcher. By pitcher handling, I mean studying opposing batters, game calling, understanding pitcher abilities and tendencies, helping the pitchers maintain focus and other duties unique to the catching position. These things are difficult to measure because we do not know how much of good or bad pitching is due to the pitcher and how much is due to the catcher. In this chapter, we will touch upon the difficulties in designing metrics to measure pitcher handling skills. We will also explore the measurement of less complex catching skills, such as controlling the running game and pitch blocking.

CATCHER ERA

In an attempt to measure pitcher handling, Bill James created the catcher ERA (CERA) statistic in the 1980s. CERA is the ERA of a team's pitching staff when a particular catcher is behind the plate. The idea is that pitching staffs should have lower ERAs when a superior defensive catcher is behind the plate.

One limitation of CERA is that different pitcher/catcher combinations do not accumulate enough innings over the course of a season for it to be considered reliable. Another concern is that it can be biased by which pitchers the catcher's catch. For example, if a catcher was the personal catcher of a team's best pitcher, his CERA would be artificially deflated by the quality of the pitcher instead of his own pitcher-handling skill. It would not be fair to compare his CERA to that of another catcher on the same team, who only caught the staff's less talented pitchers.

EARNED RUNS SAVED

To address the bias issue of CERA, John Dewan introduced the earned runs saved statistic in *The Fielding Bible – Volume II*. Simply stated, earned runs saved is the number of earned runs that a catcher saves his pitching staff. For example, Mike Mussina, of the New York Yankees had the following overall statistics in 2008:

IP	ER	ERA
200 1/3	75	3.37

Jose Molina caught 190 1/3 of Mussina's innings and the Mussin/Molina combination posted the following numbers:

IP	ER	ERA
190 1/3	68	3.22

Now, suppose Mussina actually had an ERA of 3.37 in the 190 1/3 that Molina caught. In that case, the Mussina/Molina duo would have allowed 71.3 earned runs. Subtracting the 68 actual runs allowed by the battery from 71.3 yields 3.3 earned runs saved for Molina in games pitched by Mussina. Summing Molina's earned runs saved for all the pitchers he caught yields 31 earned runs saved for the season. Because it adjusts for the quality of pitchers (based on their ERA for the season), earned runs saved is less biased than CERA. However, it is still limited by the small sample sizes for pitcher/catcher combinations.

REPEATABILITY OF PITCHER HANDLING

One of the challenges of measuring pitcher handling is that it has not yet been shown to be a repeatable skill. Keith Woolner discussed this topic in depth in *Baseball Between the Numbers* in 2006. Woolner detailed a study done by Baseball Prospectus in 1999 designed to examine CERA. For the study, they looked at every pitcher/catcher battery over a 17 year period to see if pitchers tended to work better with one catcher than they do with others on the same team. The study revealed no evidence that catchers have influence over ERA, hits walks or extra base hits. It also found no indication of catchers performing well on a yearly basis compared to their peers. Instead, CERA relative to other catchers on the same team tends to oscillate wildly throughout a catcher's career. While these results seem counter-intuitive, they have since been confirmed by multiple studies at Baseball Prospectus and elsewhere.

These findings are perplexing because so many people inside the game insist that pitcher handing is very important and that some catchers are significantly better at it than others. There may be a reason for the results due to certain limitations of the studies. One limitation of most pitcher/catcher studies is sample size. Pitchers do not start a lot of games and backup catchers, to whom starters are being compared, do not typically catch a lot of games. Thus, it is difficult to find large enough sample sizes with one year of data. It is also tricky to look at multiple years of data as team pitching staffs and back-up catchers tend to change a lot from year to year. Still, one would think that if there was a strong relationship between pitcher handling and pitcher performance, it would show up statistically somewhere. If this correlation does exist, the fact that it is so hard to detect in the data makes us question how much of a factor it is in run prevention. It's a controversial topic and one which still challenges statisticians.

OTHER CATCHER STATISTICS

While pitcher handling is difficult to quantify, some catching duties are somewhat independent of pitchers and can be measured. This includes throwing out baserunners, preventing passed balls and wild pitches, and avoiding throwing and fielding errors. Like most catcher defensive metrics, pitchers do have some influence over these rates. For example, a catcher who frequently catches a knuckleball pitcher will probably have a high number of wild pitches and passed balls. Also, since left-handed pitchers are typically better than right-handed pitchers at holding baserunners, a backstop catching a staff with lefties pitching a lot of innings will tend to have better success preventing steals. Still, the relative frequencies of stolen bases, caught stealing, wild pitches, passed balls and errors tend to be fairly consistent from year to year for many catchers, suggesting that these measures probably represent real skills.

CATCHER STOLEN BASES/ CAUGHT STEALING

Two statistics that measure the ability of catchers to control the running game are stolen bases attempted per nine innings (SBA/9) and caught stealing percentage (CS%). They are based on stolen base attempts (SBA), caught stealing (CS) and innings (Inn):

$$SBA/9 = (SBA/ Inn) \times 9$$

$$CS\% = CS/SBA$$

For example, St. Louis Cardinals catcher Yadier Molina had the following statistics in 2008:

$$Inn = 1,002$$

$$SBA = 49$$

$$CS = 15 \text{ (excludes 3 pitcher CS or pickoffs)}$$

$$SBA/9 = (49/1002) \times 9 = 0.44$$

$$CS\% = 15/49 = 0.306 \text{ or } 30.6\%$$

Molina's 0.44 SBA/9 was the best rate in the National League and his 30.6 CS% was third in the circuit.

WILD PITCHES AND PASSED PALLS

We can measure pitch blocking ability using data on wild pitches (WP) and passed balls (PB). The wild pitches plus passed balls per nine innings statistic – (WP+PB)/9 – is calculated as follows:

$$(WP+PB)/9 = ((WP + PB) / inn) \times 9$$

Wild pitches are included in this calculation, as it is often difficult to distinguish between wild pitches and passed balls and it is possible that official scorers sometimes give some catchers or pitchers the benefit of the doubt based on reputation. Since a team's pitching staff does have some influence on passed balls and wild pitches charged to catchers, this statistic should be interpreted carefully. The (WP+PB)/9 measure can easily be computed from Molina's 2008 data:

$$Inn = 1,002$$

$$WP = 34$$

$$PB = 5$$

$$(WP+PB)/9 = ((34 + 5)/1002) \times 9 = 0.350$$

Molina's 0.35 (WP+PB)/9 number was slightly better than the MLB average.

CATCHER ERRORS

Throwing errors (TE) and fielding errors (FE) made by catchers are also tracked. Those numbers can easily be converted into Throwing Errors per nine innings (TE/9) and Fielding Errors per nine innings (FE/9):

$$TE/9 = (TE/Inn) \times 9$$

$$FE/9 = (FE/Inn) \times 9$$

Yadier Molina's statistics in 2008 are shown below:

$$Inn = 1,002$$

$$TE = 7$$

$$FE = 2$$

$$FE/9 = (TE/Inn) \times 9 = (7/1,002) \times 9 = 0.063$$

$$TE/9 = (FE/Inn) \times 9 = (2/1,002) \times 9 = 0.018$$

Molina was worse than the league average on fielding errors per nine innings (.063 versus .045) and throwing errors per nine innings (.018 versus .008).

The SBA/9, CS%, (WP+PB)/9, TE and FE statistics are no longer available at HardballTimes.com but are expected to be included on FanGraphs.com by April, 2010.

CATCHER RUNS

Sean Smith was the first person known to develop a system using rates of caught stealing, wild pitches, passed balls and errors to measure catcher run prevention. We will touch upon Smith's system shortly but a somewhat simpler system will be introduced first. Inspired by Smith, Justin Inaz, who writes for BeyondTheBoxscore.com, developed his own system which we will describe with a minor tweak.

In Inaz's system, MLB averages are calculated for the following: caught stealing percentage (Lg CSRate), wild pitches plus passed balls per inning (Lg WPPBRate), throwing errors per inning (Lg TERate) and fielding errors per inning (Lg FERate):

$$Lg\ CSRate = CS/SBA$$

$$Lg\ WPPBRate = (PB + WP)/Inn$$

$$Lg\ TERate = TE/Inn$$

$$Lg\ FERate = FE/Inn$$

The MLB averages in 2008 are shown below:

$$Lg \; CSRate = .2249$$

$$Lg \; WPPBRate = .0433$$

$$Lg \; TERate = .0053$$

$$Lg \; FERate = .0011$$

We know that runners attempted to steal on Molina 49 times in 2008. Based on the .2249 Lg CSRate, we would expect the average catcher to throw out 11 runners (.2249 x 49) in 49 opportunities. Molina threw out 15 base runners attempting to steal, so his caught stealing rate above average (CS+) was +4.

Now, based on linear weights theory, the average caught stealing saves 0.63 runs (0.44 for the CS plus 0.19 for the SB not achieved). So, caught stealing runs above average (CSRuns) can be computed by multiplying CS+ by 0.63. For example, Molina had +2.52 CSRuns (4 x 0.63) in 2008. This means he saved 2.52 runs more than would be expected from the average catcher given the same opportunities.

Similar calculations can be done for WP and PB. Molina caught 1,002 innings in 2008. Based on the .0433 Lg WPPB rate, we would expect the average catcher to allow 43.4 (.0433 x 1,002) WP and PB in 1,002 innings. Molina allowed 39 WP and PB, so his WP plus PB above/below average (WPPB+) was -4.4.

Based on linear weights theory, a WP or PB costs -0.28 runs. Thus, WP plus PB above/below average is calculated by multiplying WPPB+ by -0.28. Molina had +1.23 WPPBRuns in 2008. So, he saved his team 1.23 runs more than expected in preventing wild pitches and passed balls.

Catcher throwing error runs above/below average (TERuns) are calculated the same way as WPPBRuns. A catcher throwing error typically occurs when a catcher attempts to either throw a runner out stealing or pick a runner of a base. Since the result is often similar to a WP or PB, we use the same linear weight for TE as we do for WP and PB (-0.28).

Catcher fielding error runs (FERuns) are calculated the same as WPPBRuns and TERuns except that a different linear weight is used. A catcher fielding error generally has a similar effect to errors made by other fielders (about a half run) so we use -0.50 instead of -0.28. Molina had -0.45 FERuns and -0.47 TERuns in 2008. So, he cost his team a combined 0.92 runs more than expected on errors.

Finally, all of the above run values are combined to arrive at catcher runs saved above average (CatchRuns):

$$CatchRuns = CSRuns + WPPBRuns + TERuns + FERuns$$

Yadier Molina had the following numbers in 2008:

$$
\begin{aligned}
\text{CSRuns} &= +2.52 \\
\text{WPPBRuns} &= +1.23 \\
\text{TERuns} &= -0.47 \\
\text{FERuns} &= \underline{-0.45} \\
\text{CatchRuns} &= +2.83
\end{aligned}
$$

So, by this method, Molina saved 2.83 runs more than the average catcher would have saved given the same opportunities.

Smith uses a similar method as Inaz with the following differences:

1. He adjusts for handedness of pitchers.

2. He uses SB per inning and CS per inning instead of CS%.

3. He uses the following linear weights: -0.20 for SB, +0.47 for CS, -0.275 for WP/PB/TE/FE.

Smith's results are included on Baseball-Reference.com under catcher runs above average (Rctch).

WITH OR WITHOUT YOU CATCHER DEFENSE

As noted above, catcher defense is dependent on pitchers, especially knuckleball pitchers. With this in mind, Tango used Retrosheet.org data to develop the with or without you (WOWY) method of defensive evaluation for catchers. He introduced WOWY in the *Hardball Times Annual 2008* using former Texas Rangers catcher Geno Petralli as an example. Petralli led the league in passed balls with 35 as the Rangers third-string catcher in 1987, but he was not as bad as that statistic indicated. A big part of the reason for his large number of passed balls was that the Rangers had knuckleballer Charlie Hough on their staff that year and Petralli caught 50% of his innings.

It would not be fair to evaluate Petralli against the average catcher who did not work with Hough. So, Tango determined how Hough fared with Petralli versus all other catchers. He discovered that Petralli/Hough allowed 107 PB per 5,000 batters; while others/Hough allowed 82 passed balls per 5,000 batters. Moreover, Petralli caught 94 pitchers in his career. To properly measure his defense with non-knuckleballers included, Tango repeated the process for each of those pitchers with and without Petralli. For his career, Petralli had 24 passed balls per 5,000 batters. Other catchers working with the same set of pitchers had 21 passed balls per 5,000 batters. So, Petralli allowed only three more passed balls per 5,000 batters than his comparison group.

Tango repeated the procedure he used with Petralli for all 828 catchers who played between 1957 and 2006 (except 1999 due to unavailable data at the time of the study). He also went through the same process with other statistics: stolen bases, caught stealing, pickoffs, balks and wild pitches. For each catcher, he determined how many runs they saved or cost their teams compared to their peers.

For example, former Los Angeles Dodgers catcher Steve Yeager allowed 13 fewer stolen bases per 5,000 batters than his baseline group. Additionally, he had one more caught stealing, four more pickoffs, two fewer balks, nine fewer wild pitches and three fewer passed balls. Tango assigned approximate linear weights to those events: +0.5 runs for CS and PO and -0.25 for SB, BK, WP and PB. Based on that, he determined that Yeager was 9.2 runs per 5,000 batters better than his peers during his career.

According to the WOWY system, the number one backstop, among those catching at least 15,000 batters, was Charlie O'Brien (+15.3 runs per 5,000 batters) who played for eight different teams between 1985 and 2000. The worst was Dick Dietz (-13.2) who played mostly for the San Francisco Giants between 1966 and 1973.

The WOWY method is considered by many analysts to be the most accurate assessment of catchers at this time. However, catcher defense is an area which still needs more work. While Smith, Tango, Inaz and others have begun to evaluate catcher defense, these models do not account for all aspects of catcher defense, such as handling of pitchers.

PERCENTILES

Figure 62 shows the percentiles for some of the catching statistics for MLB catchers with 500 or more innings caught in 2008. For example, it reveals that a typical CS% was 21%, 35% was very high and 15% was very low.

Figure 62: Percentiles for MLB Catchers, 2008

Percentile	SBA/9	CS%	(WP+PB)/9	TE/9	FE/9	Catch Runs
Best	0.36	43%	0.21	0.000	0.000	13.8
90%	0.52	35%	0.24	0.015	0.000	7.6
75%	0.62	28%	0.32	0.032	0.000	4.3
50%	0.76	21%	0.36	0.045	0.008	1.3
25%	0.86	18%	0.44	0.062	0.014	-1.2
10%	0.90	15%	0.48	0.074	0.020	-7.3
Worst	1.04	9%	0.52	0.137	0.029	-7.6

Data from HardballTimes.com

Chapter 13

Team Fielding

When the Tampa Bay Rays won their improbable American League pennant in 2008, their pitching staff received a good deal of attention. After giving up more runs than any team in the league in 2007, the Rays allowed the second fewest runs in 2008. An improved pitching staff anchored by starters James Shields, Matt Garza and Scott Kazmir, as well as reliever J.P. Howell certainly deserved a lot of credit for the turn around. However, the Rays defense may have played just as big of a role as the pitching in the team's dramatic improvement. Metrics that help to show the importance of the fielding to a team's success will be introduced in this chapter.

DEFENSIVE EFFICIENCY RATIO

As was the case for individual fielders, Fielding Percentage was the primary measure of team defense throughout most of baseball history. In Chapter 11, we discussed why fielding percentage is a limited measure of player defense and introduced several better defensive measures. When Bill James introduced the defensive efficiency ratio (DER) statistic in the 1978 *Baseball Abstract*, it was the first time team defense had been formerly quantified in terms of range instead of errors (E). DER is the percentage of batted balls in play, not including home runs, which are converted to outs by a team's fielders. For example, the Rays had a .710 DER in 2008 which means they turned 71 percent of balls in play into outs. The most commonly used DER formula is

$$DER = (BFP - H - K - BB - HBP - 0.6 \times E)/(BFP - HR - K - BB - HBP)$$

Note that errors are multiplied by 0.6 because, for the average team, about 60% of errors result in the failure to turn a batted ball into an out. Events such as outfielder throwing errors or errant pickoff attempts, which do not prevent a batted ball from being converted to an out, are excluded. While DER is a much better measure of team defense than fielding percentage, it fails to take several factors into consideration:

1. Types of batted balls allowed by the team's pitchers (e.g. ground balls, fly balls, line drives, bunts)

2. Location of batted balls

3. How hard the ball was hit

4. Handedness of pitcher and batter

5. Home ballpark

THE HARDBALL TIMES TEAM PLUS/MINUS STATISTIC

We discussed in Chapter 9 how pitchers have limited influence over the results of batted balls in play. Regardless of the level of control they actually do have though, some pitching staffs allow more "field-able" balls than other staffs during the course of a season, either through skill or by luck. With this is in mind, HardballTimes.com designed a new measure – the team plus/minus statistic – which incorporated batted ball type. The Hardball Times plus/minus statistic (which is not the same as the Fielding Bible plus/minus measure introduced in Chapter 11) was introduced by David Studenmund in *The Hardball Times Annual 2006*.

The Hardball Times Plus/Minus measure works as follows. First, calculate the number of each type of batted ball against a team's pitching staff. For example, suppose a hypothetical team allowed the following numbers of batted balls in a given season:

1. Ground balls = 2,000
2. Fly balls = 1,100 (not including homers)
3. Line drives = 400 (not including homers)
4. Fliners = 600 (a batted ball that's between fly ball and line drive, not including homers)
5. Pop ups = 200
6. Bunts = 100
7. Total = 4,400

Note that home runs are excluded because they are largely the responsibility of pitchers and are usually not influenced by fielders. The next step is to determine the MLB average out percentage on each type of batted ball. In a typical year, it might be:

1. Ground balls = 75%
2. Fly balls = 83%
3. Line drives = 25%
4. Fliners = 45%
5. Pop ups = 98%
6. Bunts = 78%

Using the above data, calculate the expected number of outs for our hypothetical team by multiplying the number of each batted ball type by the corresponding MLB out percentage. For example, we would expect 75% of the 2,000 ground balls allowed by this team to be outs. So, we would predict 0.75 x 2,000 = 1,500 outs on ground balls. Expected outs for other events are shown below:

1. Expected outs on Ground Balls = 1,500

2. Expected outs of Fly Balls = 913

3. Expected outs on line drives = 100

4. Expected outs on fliners = 270

5. Expected outs on pop ups = 196

6. Expected outs on bunts = 78

Summing all the expected outs for all events yields 3,057 expected outs on all batted balls in play. Now, suppose that the actual number of outs completed by this hypothetical team was 3,100. In that case, the team would be 3,100-3,057 = 43 outs above what would be expected by the average team.

ULTIMATE ZONE RATING FOR TEAMS

The Hardball Times team plus/minus statistic described above is an improvement over DER, but there are still factors which it does not consider: location of batted ball, handedness of pitcher and batter and home ballpark. In Chapter 10, we introduced a few methods for individual fielders which did incorporate these items in addition to elements which comprise the Hardball Times team plus/minus statistic. These same methods (Fielding Bible plus/minus, UZR, and PMR) can be applied to teams. The most accessible of these statistics is UZR, which is updated daily on FanGraphs.com. (Keep in mind that UZR only measures infield and outfield defense and does not yet capture pitcher and catcher defense.)

Team FIP (a measure of pitching introduced in Chapter 9) and UZR can be used to explore the association between total runs allowed and team pitching/fielding. Figure 63 below shows the relationship between runs allowed and FIP for American League teams in 2008.

Figure 63: Team FIP Vs. Runs Allowed, 2008 American League

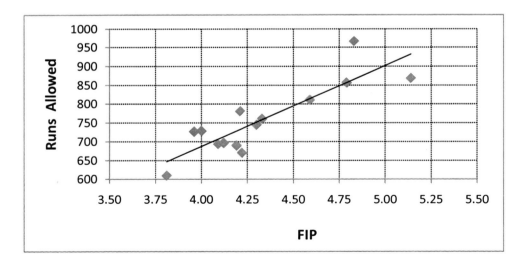

Data from FanGraphs.com

The plot shows a strong correlation between FIP and runs allowed with higher FIPs associated with higher runs allowed as expected. However, FIP does not tell the entire story of run prevention. Figure 64 below shows how the same teams ranked on FIP and UZR. We can see that the top four teams in UZR were also the top four teams in runs allowed. This suggests that fielding was also influential in run prevention.

Figure 64: Run Prevention Ranks for American League Teams, 2008

Team	RA	FIP	UZR
Toronto	1	1	4
Tampa Bay	2	8	1
Oakland	3	6	2
Boston	4	4	3
Los Angeles	5	5	8
New York	6	2	13
Chicago	7	3	11
Minnesota	8	9	9
Cleveland	9	10	5
Kansas City	10	7	6
Seattle	11	11	10
Detroit	12	12	12
Baltimore	13	14	7
Texas	14	13	14

Data from FanGraphs.com

The Rays in particular were second in the league in fewest runs allowed with 671. That was a huge improvement over 2007 when they allowed a league-worst 944 runs. That 273 run improvement explained most of their turnaround in winning percentage from 2007 to 2008. Their FIP improved from 4.70 (12th in league) in 2008 to 4.22 (8th) in 2009, which is an indication that their pitching was much improved.

While pitching was important in the rise of the Rays, their defense may have been even more crucial. After finishing a MLB worst 57.7 runs saved below average according to UZR in 2007, the Rays soared to a MLB best 74.2 runs above average in 2008. That 132-run improvement between 2007 and 2008 indicates how important defense was in their pennant run. In short, what James once said is true: "Much of what we think of as pitching is actually fielding".

OFFENSE VERSUS PITCHING VERSUS FIELDING

In Chapter 2, we looked at the relative importance of defense (pitching/fielding) and offense in reaching the postseason. It was found that good defense was slightly more important than good offense but also that a strong offensive team could win with an average defense.
I conducted a similar analysis breaking defense into pitching (FIP) and fielding (DER), while keeping runs scored as the offensive measure. It was necessary to use DER rather than UZR because UZR is only tracked back to 2002 and more years were necessary to do an adequate study.

As in Chapter 2, each facet of the game was divided into three categories according to how teams ranked on the relevant statistic. Teams that finished in the top third of the league in runs scored were classified as "Good" offensive teams; teams in the middle third were considered "OK" offensive teams; and teams in the bottom third were categorized as "Poor" offensive teams. The same categorization scheme was used for pitching (based on FIP) and for fielding (based on DER). It gets a little messy processing all three parts of the game together so they are presented separately in Figures 65-67 for the 136 playoff teams between 1988 and 2008.

Figure 65: Offensive Classification of Playoff Teams, 1988-2008

Offense	No.	%
Good	81	60
OK	45	33
Poor	10	7

Data from Baseball-Databank.org

Figure 66: Pitching Classification of Playoff Teams, 1988-2008

Pitching	No.	%
Good	84	62
OK	44	32
Poor	8	6

Data from Baseball-Databank.org

Figure 67: Fielding Classification of Playoff Teams, 1988-2008

Fielding	No.	%
Good	64	47
OK	42	31
Poor	30	22

Data from Baseball-Databank.org

Figures 65 and 66 reveal that offense and pitching were about equally important to reaching post season with 60% of playoff teams having Good offense and 62% having Good pitching. It was important for teams to be at least OK in both categories as only 7% of playoff teams had Poor offense and 6% Poor pitching. Figure 67 indicates that fielding was not quite as crucial as offense and pitching, but was still important: About half the playoff teams (47%) had Good fielding and 22% had Poor fielding.

Overall, the data suggest that offense and pitching are both key components of most winning teams and neither should be emphasized more than the other. Fielding is somewhat less vital but should not be ignored. It is wise for an organization to build a team that is strong in all three components. However, if a team has to concentrate on only two of the three, they should do so more in hitting and pitching.

Illustration by Samara Pearlstein

Chapter 14

Adjusting for Environment

A .300 batting average in today's game is not the same as a .300 batting average in 1968, the year of the pitcher. A .600 slugging average in 2000 is not equivalent to a .600 slugging average in The Deadball Era of the early 20th century. The home run total of a Colorado Rockies hitter playing in Coors Field is not comparable to the home run total of a San Diego Padres batter playing in pitcher friendly Petco Park. When we compare players from different eras, leagues and home ballparks, these different contexts need to be considered. In this chapter, we will explore how to adjust for environment to make fair evaluations of players.

LEAGUE RELATIVE STATISTICS

Boston Red Sox Hall of Famer Carl Yastrzemski led the American League with a .301 BA in 1968. Four decades later in 2007, Los Angeles Angels shortstop Orlando Cabrera finished with the same .301 BA but finished 17th in the American League. The reason for the discrepancy in their BA ranks was the difference in hitting environments between 1968 and 2007.

After an all time low .230 BA in the American League in 1968, MLB made two important rule changes in an effort to increase offense. They lowered the maximum height of the pitcher's mound from 15 inches to 10 inches and shrunk the strike zone from the area between the knees and shoulders to the area between the top of the knees and armpits. These changes – along with the creation of the designated hitter rule, smaller parks and other factors – created a much better atmosphere for hitters over time. As a result, the American League BA had increased to .271 by 2007. We can adjust for the change in league BA(Lg BA) by calculating a relative batting average for each player:

$$\text{Relative BA} = (\text{BA}/\text{Lg BA}) \times 100.$$

A more precise version of the formula removes the at bats and hits of the player in question from Lg BA but this extra layer of complexity is not necessary for most purposes. Yastrzemski had a Relative BA of (.301/.230) = 1.31 in 1968 meaning that his BA was 31% better than the league average BA. Cabrera, on the other hand, had a Relative BA of (.301/.271) = 1.11 in 2007 indicating that he was only 11% above the league average. Of course, a player can also be below league average. Light hitting Detroit Tigers shortstop Ray Oyler batted .135 in 1968 giving him a Relative BA of 0.59. This means that Oyler was 1.00-0.59=0.41 or 41% below league average. Similar calculations can be made to get relative on-base percentage, relative slugging average and other relative batting statistics.

BALLPARK FACTORS

Just as different leagues have different levels of offense, ballparks are also not created equal. For example, the Coors Field launching pad in Colorado is favorable for both BA and power, while PETCO Park in San Diego is unfavorable for all types of hitters. For this reason, it is not fair to directly compare the statistics of a Rockies hitter to a Padres hitter. For example, consider the 2007 batting lines for Padres first baseman Adrian Gonzalez and Rockies third baseman Garrett Atkins displayed in Figure 68.

Figure 68: Adrian Gonzalez vs. Garrett Atkins, 2007

Player	Team	BA	OBP	SLG	OPS
Adrian Gonzalez	SD	.282	.347	.502	.849
Garrett Atkins	COL	.301	.367	.486	.853

Source: Baseball-Reference.com

Atkins had a higher BA than Gonzlez by 19 points, but he also had the benefit of playing half of his games in a much better hitter's park. A park-adjusted BA is similar to a relative BA, but it is adjusted according to how much a batter's home park typically inflates or deflates a player's BA.

Park effects are determined by comparing the performance of each team in its home park relative to its performance on the road. A park factor (PF) is calculated to be unaffected by team make-up as much as possible. For example, a team with strong hitting and weak pitching should not unduly inflate the ballpark factor of a neutral park.

A precise calculation of park effects can be complicated, but a simple version is presented here. To obtain the Coors Field PF for BA, one must compute the BA for the Rockies and their opponents in games played at Coors Field. That number is then compared to the BA for the Rockies and their opponents in games played outside of Coors Field. More concretely, The BA PF is a simple three step process:

BA in home park = (BA at home + BA against at home)/2

BA in road parks = (BA on road + BA against on road)/2

BA PF = (BA in home park/BA in road parks)

For example, the Rockies had the following statistics for 2007:

BA at home = .298

BA against at home = .274

BA on road = .261

BA against on road = .259

Those numbers can then be plugged into the three step PF formula to get the BA PF for Coors Field:

$$\text{Total BA in home park} = (.298 + .274)/2 = .286$$

$$\text{Total BA on road} = (.261 + .259)/2 = .260$$

$$\text{BA Park Factor} = (.286/.260) = 1.10$$

The resulting 1.10 BA PF tells us that Coors Field inflated a typical player's BA by 10 percent compared to the average park in 2007. Since PF tends to vary quite a bit from year to year for the same park, a one year PF is usually not a reliable indicator of the park's true effect on hitters and pitchers. Thus, it is advisable to consider three to five years of data before applying a PF to player statistics. Using data provided by The *Bill James Handbook*, the BA PF in Coors from 2005-2009 were:

2005	2006	2007	2008	2009
1.18	1.11	1.10	1.07	1.12

The average PF over the five year period was 1.12, so we can say that Coors Field inflated BA by about 12% on average. On the other hand, Petco Park's 0.90 BA PF tells us that Petco deflated BA by about 10% on average. Similar factors can be computed for OBP and SLG and other statistics, including total runs. A player only plays half of his games in his home park, so the park factor is only applied to those games. The rest of his games are assumed to average to a neutral park factor. Based on that, one can calculate the ballpark relative BA of Gonzalez and Atkins as follows:

$$\text{Ballpark relative BA} = (BA + BA/PF)/2$$

$$\text{Gonzalez} = (.282 + .282/.90)/2 = .298$$

$$\text{Atkins} = (.301 + .301/1.12)/2 = .285$$

So, if Gonzalez and Atkins had played all of their home games in a neutral park we would estimate that Gonzalez would have out hit him .298 to .285. By adjusting for home parks, Gonzalez goes from being 19 BA points behind Atkins to 13 BA points ahead of him.

ON-BASE PLUS SLUGGING PLUS (OPS+)

In order to compare players from different leagues, seasons and ballparks at the same time, relative batting statistics and park factors described above can be combined to yield adjusted BA (BA+), adjusted OBP (OBP+) and other similar measures. The most popular statistic in this family is OPS+, which is OPS adjusted for league average and home ballpark. Before computing OPS+ for a batter, one must first calculate league-relative OBP and league-relative SLG and combine them to get league-adjusted OPS (Lg Adj OPS). Then the PF for runs can be applied to arrive at OPS+:

$$\text{Lg Adj OPS} = 100 \times (OBP/\text{Lg OBP} + SLG/\text{Lg SLG} - 1)$$

$$\text{OPS+} = (\text{Lg Adj OPS} + \text{Lg Adj OPS}/PF)/2$$

Atkins had the following numbers in 2007:

$$OBP = .367$$

$$SLG = .486$$

$$LG\ OBP\ (not\ including\ pitchers) = .341$$

$$LG\ SLG\ (not\ including\ pitchers) = .436$$

$$PF\ for\ Runs = 1.15$$

$$Lg\ Adj\ OPS = 100\ x\ (.367/.341 + .486/.436 - 1) = 119$$

$$OPS+ = (119 + 119/1.15)/2 = 111$$

In general, an OPS+ of 100 is average, an OPS+ of more than 100 is above average and an OPS+ of less than 100 is below average. So, we can say that Atkins was above average in 2007 after adjusting for league average and ballpark.

There is a popular misconception that OPS closely matches the ratio of a player's OPS to league OPS. Because of the addition of OBP and SLG in the Lg Adj OPS formula, Lg Adj OPS is not calculated relative to league average OPS. In effect, a hitter that is good in both categories – OBP and SLG – gets extra credit for both. For example, if a hitter playing in a neutral park is 25% better than league average in both OBP and SLG, he will have an OPS+ of 150. That does not mean that he is 50% more productive than the league average hitter. It would be more accurate to say that he was 25% more productive than league average.

OPS+ is most often used to compare players from different eras. For example, Figure 69 lists four players, in four different years, which hit for similar OPS (all between .918-.924) but had very different OPS+ values. St. Louis Browns outfielder George Stone led the American League at the height of the Deadball Era with a .918 OPS in 1906. Ninety-two years later in the offense-oriented 1998 season, all-star third baseman Alex Rodriguez's .921 OPS was only 14th best in the American League. The reason for the inconsistency in OPS ranks between Stone and Rodriguez was the wildly different offensive environments of the two seasons: the league OPS was .621 in 1906 and .774 in 1998.

Figure 69: OPS Comparison of Players from Different Eras

Player	Year	Lg	OPS	Rank	Lg OPS	OPS+
George Stone	1906	AL	.918	1	.621	195
Carl Yastrzemski	1968	AL	.924	1	.639	168
Mike Schmidt	1984	NL	.924	1	.691	155
Alex Rodriguez	1998	AL	.921	14	.774	135

Source: Baseball-Reference.com

EARNED RUN AVERAGE PLUS (ERA+)

Pitching statistics can also be adjusted according to league average and home ballpark. The most commonly used adjusted pitching measure is earned run average plus (ERA+) found at Baseball-Reference.com. Like OPS+, ERA+ involves a two step formula with league-adjusted ERA (Lg Adj ERA) calculated first:

$$Lg\ Adj\ ERA = (Lg\ ERA/Pitcher\ ERA) \times 100$$

$$ERA+ = (Lg\ Adj\ ERA + Lg\ Adj\ ERA \times PF)/2$$

Notice that, in the Lg Adj ERA formula, the Lg ERA goes in the numerator and the pitcher ERA in the denominator, which is the opposite of the offensive statistics above. This means that a pitcher with a below average ERA will have an ERA+ of greater than 100. This was done to stay consistent with the "bigger is better" concept of OPS+ and other adjusted statistics.

Let's use San Diego Padres right-hander Jake Peavy's 2007 season as an example:

$$ERA = 2.54$$

$$Lg\ ERA = 4.43$$

$$PF\ for\ runs = 0.80$$

$$Lg\ Adj\ ERA = (4.43/2.54) \times 100 = 174$$

$$ERA+ = (174 + 174 \times .80)/2 = 157$$

Peavy's 157 ERA+ indicates that his ERA was better than the league average pitcher after adjusting for league and home ballpark. Peavy's ERA was not 57% better than average however. The Lg Adj ERA formula compares the league ERA relative to Peavy's ERA. In order to see how Peavy performed relative to the league average, it is necessary to take the reciprocal of ERA+ and then subtract from 100. The reciprocal of 157 is: (100/157) = 0.64 or 64%. So, Peavy was 100-64 =36% better than league average after adjusting for league and ballpark.

An ERA+ below 100 would indicate that a pitcher was below league average. For example,. Philadelphia Phillies right-hander Adam Eaton posted a 73 ERA+ in 2007. Taking the reciprocal, yields 100/73 = 1.37. This tells us that Eaton was 37% worse than league average.

Now, let's go through a similar four player comparison for ERA+ as we did for OPS+ above. Figure 70 lists four players from very different environments who had similar ERAs (all between 2.63 and 2.65). St. Louis Cardinals hurler Buster Brown had a 2.64 ERA in1906 finishing 21st in the National League. Nearly a century later, the legendary Roger Clemens led the American League with a 2.65 ERA pitching for the Blue Jays in 1998. As was the case for OPS, the incongruent rankings for similar ERAs were due to the very different contexts of the two years. In 1906, the league ERA was 2.62 and in 1998, it was more than two runs higher at 4.65. While Brown's 99 ERA+ indicates that he was 1% worse than league average in 1906, Clemens was 43% better than league average in 1998.

Figure 70: ERA Comparison of Players from Different Eras

Player	Year	Lg	ERA	Rank	Lg ERA	ERA+
Buster Brown	1906	NL	2.64	21	2.62	99
Ferguson Jenkins	1968	NL	2.63	14	2.99	120
Bob Welch	1983	NL	2.65	3	3.63	136
Roger Clemens	1998	AL	2.65	1	4.65	176

Source: Baseball-Reference.com

PERCENTILES

Figure 71 shows the percentiles of OPS+ for batters with at least 400 PA and ERA+ for pitchers with at least 15 starts in 2007. For example, it reveals that the median OPS+ among regulars was 105 with 121 being very good and 91 being sub-par. Similarly, the median ERA+ for starting pitchers in 2007 was 98 with 114 or better being very good and under 84 being poor. Some readers might wonder why the ERA+ for regular starting pitchers would be below 100. The reason is because in computing ERA+, a starting pitcher is compared to both starters and relievers and the average ERA for starters is higher than that for relievers.

Figure 71: Percentiles for OPS+ and ERA+, 2007

Percentile	OPS+	ERA+
Best	177	155
90%	136	127
75%	121	114
50%	105	98
25%	91	84
10%	77	74
Worst	49	59

Data from Baseball-Reference.org

WRAP-UP

The adjustments for the different contexts of various years, leagues and parks presented in this chapter give us a more complete picture of a player's overall performance. In the next chapter we will add these adjustments to everything else we know about evaluation of offense, pitching and fielding and arrive at statistics that allow us to rank players according to everything they do on the field.

Chapter 15

Total Player Contribution

Albert Pujols was the most productive batter in the game in 2008. Ichiro Suzuki and Colorado Rockies speedster Willy Taveras were among the leading base runners. Oakland Athletics second baseman Mark Ellis and Minnesota Twins center fielder Carlos Gomez were two of the best fielders. Cliff Lee and San Francisco Giants right-hander Tim Lincecum were two of the finest starting pitchers. Mariano Rivera was arguably the top reliever. All of these players used their skills to help their teams win games. Which player helped his team the most? In this chapter, we will discuss how to combine everything we know about a player in order to estimate his total contribution to his team's win total.

WIN SHARES

The win shares system was introduced in *Win Shares,* written by Bill James and Jim Henzler in 2002. This system was the first formal attempt to estimate how many wins a player contributed to his team based on everything he does in games – batting, pitching, fielding and baserunning. The win shares algorithm allows us to compare the relative values of players at different positions, in different home ballparks and in different eras.

The methodology of win shares is very complex so only the basics are covered here. First, a team receives three win shares (WS) for every actual win during a season. For example, the Philadelphia Phillies won 92 games in 2008, so they were assigned 276 WS. Those WS were distributed among players – Chase Utley 30, Ryan Howard 24, Jimmy Rollins 24, Cole Hamels 18, etc. The quality of a team should not affect individual WS. That is, a good player on an excellent team should have about the same number of WS as an equally good player on a poor team.

James multiplied by three in the WS calculation because he wanted player contribution to be summarized by one integer which would allow us to distinguish between players. For example, if we did not use multiples of three, then three players with win shares of 6.6, 7.0 and 7.4 would round to 7 win shares. In multiplying by three, the three players would be credited with 20, 21 and 22 WS respectively.

There are three types of WS: batting, pitching and fielding. A team's WS are first divided into these three categories. Team batting WS are determined by runs scored. Those are apportioned to individuals based on theoretical team runs created (Chapter 4) and outs made. The most recent version of runs created (detailed in The 2009 *Bill James Handbook*) is used. This means that almost every element of a team's offense is considered including hits, total bases, walks, sacrifice flies, sacrifice bunts, double plays, stolen bases, caught stealing and batting average with runners in scoring position.

Team WS are apportioned to pitching through fielding independent events (walks, strikeouts, hit batsmen and home runs). For individual pitchers, the following statistics are considered:

1. Strikeouts

2. Bases on balls

3. Home runs

4. Component ERA

5. Wins and losses

6. Saves

7. High leverage innings for relievers

Team WS are apportioned to fielding through defensive efficiency ratio, passed balls, errors and double plays for fielders. For individual fielders, the following statistics are considered:

1. Caught stealing, errors, passed balls and sacrifice hits allowed for catchers

2. Double plays, assists, putouts and errors for infielders

3. Putouts, team defensive efficiency ratio, assists and errors for outfielders

These statistics are adjusted for handedness and ground ball/fly ball tendencies of pitching staffs. Play-by-play data are not used, so the resulting statistics are not as accurate as plus/minus or ultimate zone rating. The fielding measures used in the win shares system are more akin to adjusted range factor. The plus/minus, UZR and adjusted range factor statistics are covered in detail in Chapter 11.

In the end, we have the same three types of WS for individuals as for teams: batting, pitching and fielding. Batting accounts for a little less than half the WS and pitching and fielding a little more than half. Position players tend to have more WS than pitchers, because they get credit for both batting and fielding. Players at the more demanding defensive positions – catcher and shortstop, for example – are credited extra WS that players at less demanding positions do not receive. This allows us to more accurately compare the values of two players who play different positions. Win shares are also adjusted for ballparks and league averages, which allows us to compare across leagues and eras.

The win shares system is great for looking at player contributions in the past season or seasons. It is less useful for projecting forward because it includes factors such as BA with runners in scoring position, saves and individual pitcher wins that are quite variable from year to year and thus not reliable for prediction (See the repeatable statistics sections of Chapters 3 and 7). It is useful for determining Most Valuable Player and Cy Young award winners, assessing Hall of Fame credentials and evaluating trades. For a more detailed summary of the win shares system, consult James's *Win Shares* or David Studenmund's BaseballGraphs.com site.

Figure 72 shows that Joe Mauer led the American League with 30 WS in 2008. This means that he contributed an estimated 10 wins to the Twins. Some analysts consider 20 WS to be all-star level performance, 30 WS to be MVP caliber and 40+ WS to be an historic exceptional season. Figure 72 also tells us that three American League players had more WS than MVP winner Dustin Pedroia in 2008.

Figure 72: American League Win Shares Leaders, 2008

Player	WS
Joe Mauer	30
Justin Morneau	28
Kevin Youkilis	27
Dustin Pedroia	26
Josh Hamilton	26
Grady Sizemore	26

Source: Bill James Handbook 2009, pg. 432

Figure 73 tells us that Houston Astros first baseman Lance Berkman finished with more WS than National League MVP winner Albert Pujols. That is because Berkman logged more playing time than Pujols – 159 games versus 148 games. This example highlights what many analysts feel is a shortcoming of the win shares system. Even a poor player can accumulate WS, if he gets enough at bats or plays enough innings. The result is that the win shares system may give too much credit for playing time in general.

Figure 73: National League Win Shares Leaders, 2008

Player	WS
Lance Berkman	36
Albert Pujols	34
Hanley Ramirez	32
Chase Utley	30
Carlos Beltran	29

Source: Bill James Handbook 2009, pg. 432

The win shares system is a reasonable tool for estimating the contributions of Hall of Fame candidates. According to *Total Baseball Encyclopedia*, edited by John Thorn in 2004, Hall of Fame inductee Jim Rice had just the 12th highest WS total among 2009 Hall of Fame candidates (Figure 74). So, if you heard some grumbling from the sabermetrics community about Rice making the Hall of Fame, that is one of the reasons.

Figure 74: Win Shares for Hall of Fame Candidates, 2009

Player	WS
Rickey Henderson	535
Tim Raines	390
Mark McGwire	342
Andre Dawson	340
Bert Blyleven	339

Dave Parker	327
Alan Trammell	318
Harold Baines	307
Dale Murphy	294
Mark Grace	294
Tommy John	289
Jim Rice	282

Source: Total Baseball, 2004

WINS ABOVE REPLACEMENT

More recently, Tom Tango developed the wins above replacement (WAR) statistic. WAR is similar to WS in that it tells us how many wins a player contributes to his team. However, it is somewhat simpler to calculate. It is also more accurate than WS due, in part, to the use of UZR for estimation of runs saved by fielders. In simple terms, WAR is the wins a player contributed to his team's win total above what you would expect from a replacement level player – a theoretical player who could be acquired for league minimum salary. An example of a replacement player would be a player in AAA, who is good enough to get some time in the majors, but is not regarded as a top prospect.

The WAR statistic combines the offensive and defensive contributions of a position player. The WAR hitting component is weighted runs above average (Chapter 5) adjusted for the effect of each player's home park. The WAR fielding component is UZR (Chapter 11). FanGraphs.com has not yet chosen a fielding metric for catchers. For the time being, all catchers are treated as average defensively.

The WAR system also adjusts for a player's position. For example, shortstops have more difficult jobs and are scarcer commodities than first basemen. So, an average shortstop is worth more runs defensively than an average first baseman. Based on the fielding performance of players who played multiple positions, points are added or subtracted to a player's fielding runs total based on the difficulty of his position:

C +12.5 per 162 g

1B -12.5

2B +2.5

3B +2.5

SS +7.5

LF -7.5

CF +2.5

RF -7.5

DH -17.5

The wRAA and UZR values and positional adjustment are summed to get total player runs above average (RAA). In order to convert RAA to runs above a replacement (RAR), we need to add runs to each player's total. Because the typical replacement player is considered to be 20 runs below average over a full season, 20 runs per 600 plate appearances are added to a player's total. For example, if a player has 600 PA, then 20 will be added to his run value. If he has only 300 PA, then 10 will be added. The result is that players with more playing time will get credit for their durability. FanGraphs.com provides the following statistics:

1. Batting – wRAA

2. Fielding – UZR

3. Replacement – Runs added for replacement value

4. Positional – Position adjustment

5. RAR (value runs) = Batting + Fielding + Replacement + Positional

Based on Pete Palmer's theory that ten additional runs is worth one win to a team (Chapter 2), RAR is divided by 10 to get WAR or Value Wins. One can compute value statistics for Florida Marlins shortstop Hanley Ramirez using data from his 2008 season:

1. Batting = 46.6

2. Fielding = -0.7

3. Replacement = 23.1

4. Position = +6.9 (based on 150 games at shortstop)

5. RAR = 46.6 – 0.7 + 23.1 + 6.9 = 75.9

6. WAR (value wins) = 75.9/10=7.6

Thus, we can say that Ramirez was worth 7.6 wins more than a replacement level player. The Top WAR values among American League and National League hitters in 2008 are shown in Figures 75 and 76 respectively. Appropriately, the players with the highest WAR values in their respective leagues also won the MVP awards. So, based on the WAR statistic, the voters made reasonable choices for these awards in 2008.

Figure 75: American League WAR Leaders, 2008

Player	WAR
Dustin Pedroia	6.6
Grady Sizemore	6.3
Nick Markakis	6.2
Alex Rodriguez	6.0
Joe Mauer	5.9

Source: FanGraphs.com

Figure 76: National League WAR Leaders, 2008

Player	WAR
Albert Pujols	8.9
Chase Utley	8.1
Hanley Ramirez	7.6
Chipper Jones	7.6
David Wright	7.4

Source: FanGraphs.com

For years prior to 2002 where UZR data are not available, a different version of WAR needs to be used. Sean Smith calculated WAR using a similar methodology as above but he uses an adjusted range factor for 1871-1953 and Total Zone for 1954-2009. Results for 1955-2001 may be somewhat less accurate than those since 2002 due to less detailed retrosheet.org data. Numbers prior to 1954 will certainly be less reliable than later years. Smith's final WAR estimates can be found at BaseballProjection.com for all players in all years since 1871.

Smith's historical WAR estimates add to debates about which players should or should not be in the Hall of Fame. Figure 77 lists the top players according to WAR, who are eligible for the Hall of Fame but who have not yet been elected. All seven have WAR values in the top 75 in the history of the game. This means that they have more WAR than over half the position players currently in the Hall of Fame. These numbers support the arguments of fans who believe that players such as long time Tigers second baseman Lou Whitaker and Cubs third baseman Ron Santo should be getting more Hall of Fame consideration

Figure 77: Top Seven WAR Among Hall of Fame-Eligible Players

Player	Years	WAR
Bill Dahlen	1891-1911	75.9
Lou Whitaker	1977-1995	69.6
Barry Larkin	1986-2004	68.8
Bobby Grich	1970-1986	67.6
Edgar Martinez	1987-2004	67.2
Alan Trammell	1977-1996	66.8
Ron Santo	1960-1974	66.4

Source: BaseballProjection.com

WAR Pitching is more complicated than its hitting counterpart, so it is only covered briefly here. For a more detailed discussion, consult David Cameron's series of *Win Values Explained* articles on FanGraphs.com. First, understand that the pitcher version of wRAA is based on the FIP statistic (Chapter 9), but it is scaled to runs per game rather than ERA and is adjusted for ballpark.

The replacement level is different for starters and relievers. In general, relievers have an easier job than starters because they only have to pitch an inning or two, can throw their hardest in that time and are often used to pitch to specific batters. In fact, many relievers are failed starters. In 2008, the following replacement FIP values were used:

4.68 for A.L. relievers

5.63 for A.L. starters

4.45 for N.L. relievers

5.37 for N.L. starters

A pitcher's FIP is compared to replacement level FIP to get RAR. RAR is then converted to wins. For pitchers, run environments change depending on the pitcher. For example, Cleveland Indians left hander Cliff Lee lowered his run environment every time he pitched in 2008 because fewer runs were typically scored in games that he pitched. This means it won't take 10 runs to add one win for every pitcher. It might be 8.8 for a good pitcher and 11.2 for a weaker pitcher.

Relievers also get credit for pitching in high leverage situations (Chapter 10). This is because runs allowed by relievers tend to have a different impact on wins than runs allowed by starters. The following statistics can be found at FanGraphs.com:

1. Starting – RAR as a starter

2. Starting IP – IP as starter

3. Relieving – RAR as a reliever

4. Relieving IP – IP as a reliever

5. Total RAR (value runs) = Starting + Relieving

6. WAR (value wins)

San Francisco Giants hurler Tim Lincecum had the following WAR statistics in 2008:

1. Starting = 67.2

2. Start IP = 223.0

3. Relieving = 0.2

4. Relief IP = 4.0

5. RAR = 67.4

6. WAR = 7.5

Thus, Lincecum was 7.5 wins better than a replacement player in 2008. The WAR leaders among American League and National League pitchers in 2008 are shown in Figures 78 and 79 respectively. Here, American League Cy Young Award winner Cliff Lee finished in second place and National League winner Tim Lincecum finished first. Just as they did for MVP Awards, the voters made reasonable choices for the Cy Young awards in 2008 according to the WAR statistic.

Figure 78: American League WAR Pitching Leaders, 2008

Player	WAR
Roy Halladay	7.4
Cliff Lee	7.2
Ervin Santana	5.8
AJ Burnett	5.5
Mike Mussina	5.3

Source: FanGraphs.com

Figure 79: National League WAR Pitching Leaders, 2008

Player	WAR
Tim Lincecum	7.5
Danny Haren	6.5
Brandon Webb	6.1
Ryan Dempster	5.1
Derek Lowe	4.9

Source: FanGraphs.com

WINS ABOVE REPLACEMENT PLAYER (WARP)

The WAR statistic at FanGraphs.com is not the only one of its kind. The wins above replacement player (WARP) statistic was created by analyst Clay Davenport and is owned by Baseball Prospectus. It uses a similar methodology and is interpreted the same way as the WAR statistic described above. For example, Hanley Ramirez had a WARP of 8.2 in 2008, so he was about 8 wins better than a replacement-level player. WARP is different from WAR in that it has Baseball Prospectus proprietary methods as the base of its calculation.

WARP for position players is based on Equivalent Average (Chapter 4) and the Baseball Prospectus fielding-runs statistic. Their fielding measure is computed using a similar methodology to UZR but it uses less-detailed play-by-play data. The reason a less sophisticated fielding measure is used for WARP is that Davenport wants to evaluate major and minor league players using the same metric and minor league fielding data is not as complete as major league fielding data. While this practice facilitates translation of minor league performance into MLB performance, it also potentially makes WARP a less accurate player win estimator.

Pitcher WARP is based on defense-adjusted ERA (DERA), a statistic which adjusts for the quality of team defense supporting a pitcher while he is in the game. DERA helps to put a pitcher backed by weak fielders on even ground with a pitcher surrounded by stellar defenders. This unique feature of DERA is the biggest difference between WARP and WAR for pitchers. While WAR assumes that a pitcher has no effect on balls in play, WARP attempts to divide the responsibility of batted balls in play between pitchers and hitters.

TOTAL RUNS

The total runs statistic developed James and John Dewan and introduced in *The Fielding Bible – Volume II* is structured similarly to WAR and WARP. However, it is given in absolute runs instead of wins above replacement. It is based on the following components:

1. Theoretical runs created using technical RC (Chapter 4)

2. Defensive runs saved (Chapter 11)

3. Positional adjustments based on difficulty of position and innings played (e.g. 36 runs for full-time shortstops and 13 runs for full-time first basemen)

4. Baserunning runs (Chapter 7)

The above totals are summed to get total runs. For example, Philadelphia Phillies second baseman Chase Utley had the following numbers in 2008:

$$RC = 122$$

$$\text{Defensive runs saved} = +34$$

$$\text{Positional adjustment} = +31$$

$$\text{Baserunning runs} = +5$$

$$\text{Total Runs} = 192$$

Chase Utley had 192 total runs in 2008. This says that he contributed an estimated 192 runs with his batting, baserunning and fielding. That was the highest total in MLB in 2008. Results for all players can be found at BillJamesOnline.com. Dewan has not yet developed a pitching companion for total runs.

WHICH METHOD SHOULD WE USE?

Which of the options presented in this chapter is best for summarizing total player value? For position players, I recommend the WAR statistic because it is based on the strong combination of weighted runs above average and ultimate zone rating. I believe that the weighted runs above average measure has a stronger theoretical foundation (linear weights) than any of the batting statistics used in WS, WAR or total runs. In addition, UZR is more advanced than the fielding measures used by WARP or WS. One small advantage of the total runs method over WAR is that it adds baserunning runs beyond stolen bases.

The limitation of WAR is that UZR based WAR values are only available back to 2002. If one wants to evaluate players from previous years, total zone based WAR, WARP or WS can be used.

There is no consensus among analysts as to which method is best for the evaluation of pitchers, although it is generally believed that WAR and WARP are more accurate than WS. Because there is still uncertainty as to how run prevention should be divided between pitchers and fielders, analysts are more hesitant about the use of a catch all statistic for pitcher performance.

So, in the case of pitchers, it's even more important to consider a variety of statistics in performance evaluation.

RECOMMENDATIONS

While it is nice to have one number which summarizes a player's season, we should remember that relying solely on a single value to define a player is generally not a good idea. It is important to understand a player's strengths and weaknesses, which contributed to his final win estimate. The more we know about a player, the more we understand his value to his particular team. For example, a great fielding, poor hitting shortstop might have more value to a team with an otherwise strong offense than to a team with a weak offense.

Additionally, the more data we have on a player, the easier it is to forecast his future performance. For example, a player whose total value is based primarily on a non-repeatable measure, such as batting average, might have a more difficult time sustaining his performance than a player who relies more on walks and slugging. Therefore, it is desirable to look at a number of batting, baserunning, fielding and pitching statistics in evaluating a player's season. How many measures one should incorporate in an analysis depends on what questions one is answering and how complex one wishes to get.

To measure batting, I suggest PA, BA, ISO, BB%, BB/K ratio, OPS and wOBA. It is also important to remember that player performance varies significantly from year to year. Thus, it is desirable to look at two or three year averages for each statistic. All of these measures can be found at FanGraphs.com for one, two, three years or an entire career.

For baserunning, I recommend SB, CS and the equivalent baserunning statistics (EqBRR and EqSBR). If one wants to determine a player's baserunning contribution beyond base stealing, then he or she can subtract EqSBR from EqBRR. These measures can be found at BaseballProspectus.com.

For fielders, I like to take an average of the best advanced fielding measures available. That includes UZR (FanGraphs.com), plus/minus (BillJamesOnline.com), Rtz (Baseball-Reference.com) and PMR (BaseballMusings.com). The Fan Scouting report at TangoTiger.net is another valuable resource. It is especially important to consider multiple years of data when evaluating fielders.

I propose IP, K/9, BB/9, GB%, ERA, FIP, and BABIP in evaluating pitchers. In addition to those statistics, I suggest WPA for relievers. All of these metrics can be found at FanGraphs.com.

THE LAST WORD

Baseball statistics have come a long way since the first box score in 1845, but the evolution is not complete. In this book, I have introduced most of the measures I think knowledgeable fans should be aware of for the coming seasons, but there is still more to learn about the game. Some of the more advanced metrics described in this book will find their way into the mainstream, the way statistics such as OPS and WHIP have in recent years. Other measures will become staples in the sabermetric community, but may never reach the majority of fans. There will also no doubt be new and improved statistics to replace some of the current measures.

Much is being done to advance the science of sabermetrics even further. For example, cameras installed in every major league park are tracking the precise speed, location and other characteristics of every pitch. Additional cameras will be installed in 2010 which will give us more information on batters and fielders as well. This technology will surely lead us to a greater understanding of the game than was previously possible. Indeed, the sabermetrics journey is far from complete.

Bibliography

Albert, Jim (2003). *Curve Ball*. New York, NY: Springer-Verlag.

Baseball Info Solutions, James, Bill (2009). *The Bill James Handbook 2009*. Skokie, IL: ACTA Sports.

Boswell, Tom (1981). Baseball's Best Stat, *Inside Sports*. January, 1981

Codell, Barry (1979), The Base-Out Percentage: Baseball's Newest Yardstick. *Baseball Research Journal*, 35-39.

Cook, Earnshaw (1964). *Percentage Baseball*. Cambridge, MA: MIT Press.

Costa, Gabriel, Huber, Michael and Saccoman, John (2008). *Understanding Sabermetrics*. Jefferson, NC: McFarland & Company, Inc.

Cramer, Richard (1977). Do Clutch Hitters Exist? The Baseball Research Journal, SABR, 6(1)

Deford, Frank (1964). Baseball is Played All Wrong. *Sports Illustrated*, 20(12), 14-17.

Dewan, John, Callis, Jim, Zminda, Don (2000). *Baseball Scoreboard*. Morton Grove, IL: STATS, Inc.

Dewan, John (2009). *The Fielding Bible Volume II*. Skokie, IL: ACTA Sports.

Dolphin, Andrew (2004). Clutch Hitting: Fact or Fiction? Februrary 2, 2004, *Dolphin Rankings*: http://www.dolphinsim.com/ratings/notes/clutch.html

Gillette, Gary, and Palmer, Pete (2008). *The ESPN Baseball Encyclopedia Fifth Edition*. New York, NY: Sterling Publishing Co.

James, Bill (1984). *The Bill James Baseball Abstract*. New York, NY: Ballantine Books.

James, Bill (1985). *The Bill James Baseball Abstract*. New York, NY: Ballantine Books.

James, Bill (1986). *The Bill James Baseball Abstract*. New York, NY: Ballantine Books.

James, Bill (2001). *The Bill James Historical Baseball Abstract*. New York, NY: The Free Press.

James, Bill, Henzler, Jim (2002). *Win Shares*. Morton Grove, IL: STATS, Inc.

Jazayerli, Rany, Woolner, Keith (1999). Bullpens: The Last Word. July 8, 1999, *Baseball Prospectus: http://www.baseballprospectus.com/article.php?articleid=347*

Kahrl, Christina, Goldman, Steven, and The Baseball Prospectus team of Experts (2009). *Baseball Prospectus 2009*. New York, NY: Penguin Group.

Keri, Jonah, Click, James, Davenport, James, Demause, Neil, Goldman, Steven, Perry, Dayn, Silver, Nate, and Woolner, Keith (2006). *Baseball Between the Numbers*. New York, NY: Basic Books.

Krabbenhoft, Herm (2009). Who Invented Runs Produced? *The Baseball Research Journal*, SABR, 38(1), 135-138.

Lane, Ferdinand Cole (1916). Why the System of Batting Average Should be Changed. *Baseball Magazine*, 16, 41-47.

Lanigan, Ernest (1922). *Baseball Cyclopedia.* New York, NY: Baseball Magazine Company

Lewis, Michael (2003). *Moneyball: The Art of Winning an Unfair Game*. NewYork, NY: W.W. Norton

Lichtman, Mitchel (2004). DIPS Revisited. February 29, 2004, Baseball Think Factory: http://www.baseballthinkfactory.org/files/primate_studies/discussion/lichtman_2004-02-29_0/

Lindsey, George (1959). Statistical Data Useful for the Operation of a Baseball Team. *Operations Research*, 7,2, 197-207

Lindsey, George (1961). The Progress of the Score During a Baseball Game. *Journal of the American Statistical Association*, 56 (295), 703-728.

Lindsey, George (1963). An Investigation of Strategies in Baseball. *Operations Research*, 11 (4), 477-501.

McCracken, Voros (2001). Pitchers and Defense: How Much Control do Hurlers Have? January 23, 2001, *Baseball Prospectus:* //www.baseballprospectus.com/article.php?articleid=878

Mills, Eldon and Mills, Harlan (1970). *Player Win Averages: A Computers Guide to Winning Baseball Players*. South Brunswick, NJ: A.S. Barnes.

Neyer, Rob (2006). Quality Start Still a Good Measure of Quality. April 13, 2006, *ESPN.com:* http://inside.espn.go.com/mlb/insider/columns/story?columnist=neyer_rob&id=2407313

Okrent, Dan (1981). He Does It by the Numbers, *Sports Illustrated*, May, 1981.

Oz, Frank (1995). The Monster in the Mirror. On *Sesame Street Platinum: All Time Favorites*. New York, NY: Sony Wonder.

Palmer, Pete (1990). Clutch Hitting One More Time. *By The Numbers,* SABR, 2(2), 6-7.

Rickey, Branch (1954). Goodby to Some Old Baseball Ideas, *Life*, August 2, 1954.

Schwarz, Alan (2004). *The Numbers Game.* New York, NY: St. Martin's Press.

Seidman, Eric (2008). *Bridging the Statistical Gap.* Philadelphia, PA: Ergeniseid.

Studenmund, David, and The Hardball Times staff writers (2006). *The Hardball Times Baseball Annual 2006*. Skokie, IL: ACTA Sports.

Studenmund, David, and The Hardball Times staff writers (2007). *The Hardball Times Baseball Annual 2007*. Skokie, IL: ACTA Sports.

Studenmund, David, and The Hardball Times staff writers (2008). *The Hardball Times Baseball Annual 2008*. Skokie, IL: ACTA Sports.

Tango, Tom, Lichtman, Mitchel, Dolphin Andrew (2007). *The Book: Playing the Percentages in Baseball*. Dulles, VA: Potomac Books, Inc.

Thorn, John, Birnbaum, Phil, Deane, Bill (2004). *Total Baseball: The Ultimate Baseball Encyclopedia*. Toronto, Ontario, Canada: Sports Media Publishing.

Thorn, John, Palmer, Pete (1985). *The Hidden Game of Baseball*. Garden City, NY: Doubleday and Company, Inc.

Tippett, Tom (2002). Evaluating Defense. December 5, 2002, *Diamond-Mind.com:* http://www.diamond-mind.com/articles/defeval.htm

Tippett, Tom (2003), Can Pitchers Prevent Hits on Balls in Play? July 21, 2003, *Diamond-Mind.com:* http://www.diamond-mind.com/articles/ipavg2.htm

Woolner, Keith (2001). Introduction to VORP: Value Over Replacement Player. *StatHead.com*: http://www.stathead.com/bbeng/woolner/vorpdescnew.htm

Web Sites

Appleman, David. *FanGraphs*. http://www.fangraphs.com

Associated Press and News Corporation. *STATS*. http://www.stats.com.

Bradbury, JC. *Sabernomics*. *http*://www.sabernomics.com

Bloom, David. *Baseball Happenings*. http://www.baseballhappenings.com

Cameron, David. *U.S.S. Mariner*. http://www.ussmariner.com/

Carruth, Matthew and MacAree, Graham. *Stat Corner*. *http*::://www.statcorner.com

Dewan, John. *Baseball Info Solutions*. http://www.baseballinfosolutions.com

Dewan, John. *Fielding Bible Awards*. http://www.billjamesonline.net/fieldingbible/complete-votetally.asp

ESPN Internet Ventures. *ESPN*. http://espn.go.com/mlb/statistics

Forman, Sean and Lahman, Sean. *Baseball-DataBank*. http://www.baseball-databank.org

Gleeman, Aaron. AaronGleeman.com. http://www.aarongleeman.com.

Fox, Dan. *Dan Agonistes*. http://danagonistes.blogspot.com/

Furtado, Jim and Szymborski, Dan. *Baseball Think Factory*. http://www.baseballthinkfactory.org

Glab, Keith. *Baseball Evolution*. http://www.Baseballevolution.com

Heipp, Brandon. *Walk Like a Saber*. http://walksaber.blogspot.com

James, Bill. *Bill James Online*. http://www.billjamesonline.net

Lederer, Rich. Baseball Analysts. http://www.baseballanalysts.com

Menig, Scott. *MotownSports*. http://www.motownsports.com

Morong, Cyril. Cybermetrics. http://cybermetrics.blogspot.com

Pinto, David. *Baseball Musings*. http://www.baseballmusings.com

Prospectus Entertainment Ventures, LLC. *BaseballProspectus.com* http://www.baseballprospectus.com

Shandler, Ron. *BaseballHQ.com*. http://www.baseballhq.com

Shea, Christopher. *Walk-off balk win expectancy finder*. http://winexp.walkoffbalk.com/expectancy/search

Smith, David. *Retrosheet*. http://www.retrosheet.org.

Smith, Sean. *Baseball Projection*. http://www.baseballprojection.com

Sports Blog Nation. *Beyond the Box Score*. http://www.beyondtheboxscore.com

Sports Reference LLC. *Baseball-Reference.com – Major League Statistics and Information*. http://www.baseball-reference.com

Studenmund, David. *Major League Baseball Graphs*. http://www.baseballgraphs.com

Studenmund, David. *The Hardball Times*. http://www.hardballtimes.com

Tango, Tom. *TangoTiger.net*. http://www.tangotiger.net

Tango, Tom. *The Book Blog*. http://www.insidethebook.com/ee/

Woolner, Keith. *StatHead*. http://www.stathead.com

INDEX

LaVergne, TN USA
29 December 2010

210539LV00001B/67/P